Additions and Corrections to the W.P.A. Inventory of Allen County, Ohio: LIMA

Jana Sloan Broglin

HERITAGE BOOKS
2024

HERITAGE BOOKS
AN IMPRINT OF HERITAGE BOOKS, INC.

Books, CDs, and more—Worldwide

For our listing of thousands of titles see our website
at
www.HeritageBooks.com

Published 2024 by
HERITAGE BOOKS, INC.
Publishing Division
5810 Ruatan Street
Berwyn Heights, MD 20740

(Originally Titled)
INVENTORY OF THE COUNTY ARCHIVES OF OHIO

Prepared by
The Historical Records Survey
Division of Women's and Professional Projects
Works Progress Administration

Allen County
Lima

Columbus, Ohio
The Historical Records Survey
December 1936

International Standard Book Number
Paperbound: 978-0-7884-2766-4

TABLE OF CONTENTS

Allen County and its Records System

County Offices and their Records

PREFACE
2nd Edition

In 1929 after the stock market crash along with the Great Depression which followed, President Herbert Hoover and his successor Franklin D. Roosevelt formulated relief projects, the most successful was the establishment of the Works Progress Administration (WPA).

Established as the Works Projects Administration in 1935, the WPA was the largest of the many programs developed during Roosevelt's "New Deal." In 1939, the agency's name was changed to Works Progress Administration, and continued as such until its demise in 1943.

The Federal Writers' Project, a division of the WPA (known as Federal Project Number One), created jobs for many unemployed librarians, clerks, researchers, editors, and historians. The workers went to courthouses, town halls, offices in large cities, vital statistics offices and inventoried records. Besides indexing works, many records were transcribed. One of these many projects was the *Inventory of the County Archives* which has benefitted genealogists and historians. The inventories listed the records, either by volumes or file boxes and years per record type, within the office. Although the WPA oversaw this project, the information for each volume of records may differ significantly by the information submitted.

This project was to encompass all of Ohio's eighty-eight counties although approximately thirty of these inventories have been located while others may not have been done. The original WPA volume for Allen County contained maps showing the evolution of Ohio judicial districts and flow charts which have been omitted in this volume.

PREFACE
2nd Edition

The information herein is verbatim from the original document except for obvious spelling errors. Records listed may have met the requirement for retention and have been destroyed as per the records retention act, while other records are considered permanent records. (*See:* **https://codes.ohio.gov/ohio-revised-code** Ohio Revised Code, sections 149.31 and 149.34). Records considered "open" to the public, such as lunacy, idiotic, and juvenile cases, may be "closed" due to a revision of state laws. However, the records may be opened to family members with adequate proof of lineage.

The addresses and website section of this edition list an up-to-date location guide to each office mentioned.

Note: This series numbered the counties as they appear as listed alphabetically. Reference is made in the first preface that Allen is number one, while it is actually number two.

Jana Sloan Broglin
Fellow, Ohio Genealogical Society
Swanton, Ohio
2024

PREFACE
1st Edition

The Survey of State and Local Historical records under the national direction of Dr. Luther H. Evans began operations in Ohio in February 1936. The project was under the administrative supervision of the Federal Writers' Project. When the separation of the projects became effective nationally, the Ohio project continued under the same supervision. The purpose of the Survey was to discover, inventory, and make accessible information concerning the basic materials for research in the history of the country. The survey comprehended a descriptive inventory of public records of the state, county, and local records of churches and other social organizations.

The emphasis of the survey in Ohio has been on public archives. The plan has been to prepare an inventory of the records of each county in a condensed style, giving the limiting dates are the records and existence, a brief description of their contents, and their location in the county courthouse or other depository. The record titles are arranged either functionally or in order of importance under each office. In the index the titles are arranged alphabetically with the addition of cross references. A prefatory note to the condensed inventory of each office gives a brief history of the office based largely upon a study of the statutes.

The survey in Allen County was started in March 1936 and was completed in September, providing 30 man-months of work. Because changing of personnel necessitated by resignations to private employment and transfers to increase the efficiency of the project, a total of seven workers was employed during the progress of the inventory. Excellent cooperation on the part of the county officials aided and speeded the work in every office.

The following letter of appreciation was received from the county auditor after the inventory in his office had been completed:

"An old record that one of your writers unearthed in the Allen County courthouse made me stop and think just what the project has meant to Allen County, so I am taking time out long enough to write you in regards to this work. Not a day passed, prior to this work, but someone was in the office looking up old records; generally it was a long and tiring search ending in disappointment. Since the work has been completed, we have been able to locate those old records and furnish much valuable information to the public in general. I want to thank you for whoever was the instigator of this project, and I assure you that it is something well worthwhile."

For the completeness and accuracy of the inventory itself, the project personnel in Allen County has been entirely responsible. The state office of the survey has contributed the legal histories and the final editing of the county materials.

This *Guide to Allen County Archives* is the first of a series of volumes which will be reproduced and made available to the state and local public officials, institutions and agencies; they will constitute a complete condensed guide to all state and local public records in Ohio.

William D. Overton, Associate Director
Historical Records Survey,
Curator of History, Ohio State
Archaeological and Historical Society,
Columbus, 1936

am. . . . . amended
Arch. . . . . Archaeological
Art. . . . . Article
assizes . . . . an action, writ, or verdict
Assn . . . . Association
c.. . . . . copyright
certiorari . . . . to be more fully informed
CCC . . . . Civilian Conservation Corps
cf. . . . . (confer) compare
comp. . . . . compiler
dept. . . . . department
ed. . . . . editor
et al. . . . . (et alii), and others
(et) passim . . . . (and) here and there
ex officio. . . . . as a result of one's status or position
fee simple. . . . . full and irrevocable ownership
G.C. . . . . General Code
H. . . . . House bill
habeas corpus . . . . protection against illegal imprisonment
Hist. . . . . Historical
ibid. . . . . the same reference
I.C.H. . . . . Improved County Highways
Ill. State Bar Assn. Law Ser. . Illinois State Bar Association Law Service
L.T.B.. . . . . Lima Trust Building
Loc. Cit. (loco citato) . . . . in the place cited
mandamus . . . when an officer or authority is required to perform a duty
Mun.. . . . . Municipal
n. . . . . north
Nat.. . . . . National
n.d. . . . . no date
ne exeat . . . . a writ issued to restrain a person from leaving the jurisdiction of the court or state
N.P. . . . . The Ohio NISI PRIUS REPORTS
n.p. . . . . no place of publication
n.s. . . . . new series

ABBREVIATIONS, LEGAL TERMS, AND EXPLANATION

nolle prosequi . . . . notice of abandonment by a plaintiff or prosecutor of all or part of a suit or action
Ohio Const. . . . . Ohio Constitution
Ohio State Arch. and Hist. Quarterly. . . . . Ohio State Archives and Historical Quarterly
O. L. . . . . Ohio Laws
op. cit. (opere citato). . . . . in the work cited
O.P.O.. . . . . Old Post Office
posse comitatus . . . . a group of citizens called upon to assist the sheriff
praecipes . . . . a written request for action
prima facie. . . . . on the first impression
procedendo. . . . . sends case from appellate court to a lower court
Pt.. . . . . part
quo warranto . . . . by what authority or warrant
R. . . . . River
replevins. . . . . return of personal property wrongfully taken or held by a defendant
R.S.. . . . . Revised Statute
S.b.. . . . . senate bill
scire facias. . . . . why a judgment regarding a record or patent should not be enforced
sec(s) . . . . section(s)
Ser.. . . . . Series/Services
sic. . . . . thus, following copy
St.. . . . . Saint, Street
supersedeas . . . . . . a stay of enforcement of a judgment pending appeal
supt. . . . . superintendent
U.S. . . . . United States
v.. . . . . versus
venires . . . . a group of people summoned for jury duty
vol(s) . . . . volume(s)
writ. . . . . a formal, legal document, a decree
WPA. . . . . Works Progress Administration
X.. . . . . by
– . . . . to date, current

If a record has no title or a non-descriptive or misleading title an appropriate title has been assigned. Supplied titles have been enclosed in brackets. Explanatory additions to titles are enclosed in brackets with initial capitals.

If the title of a record varies, the current or most recent title is used but significant variations are shown in the title line.

Numbers and letters within parentheses following the quantity of the record indicate the labeling on volumes, file boxes, or bundles.

Title line cross references are used to complete series where a record is kept separately for a period of time or in other records for different periods of time. They are also used in all artificial entries which are made to show, under their proper office or subject heading, records kept in the same volume or file with unrelated records. In both instances, the description of the master entry shows the title and entry number of the record from which the cross reference is made. Dates shown in the description of the master entry are only for the part or parts of the record contained therein, and are shown only when they vary from those of the master entry.

Separate third paragraph cross references from entry to entry, and "see also" references under subject headings, are used to show prior, subsequent, related records which are not a part of the same series.

Unless an index is self-contained an entry for the index immediately follows its record entry. Cross references are given for exceptions to the rule.

If no statement is made concerning the condition of the records, it is to be assumed that they are in good condition.

Dimensions given in each entry show the size of the volumes, file boxes, or maps mentioned in the title line and are expressed in inches unless otherwise indicated. The dimensions of volumes are given in order of height, width, and thickness of file boxes in order of height, width, and depth.

On maps and plat records, the names of author and publisher, and information on scale has been omitted only when these data are not available.

Unless otherwise indicated all records are located in the county courthouse.

Title to the lands comprising Allen County has been claimed at various times by a number of different peoples. The first of those were the American Indians, who held title to the lands when the first white men arrived in the territory. Title was relinquished to the United States by the Treaty of Maumee Rapids, September 29, 1817. By this treaty the Wyandot, Shawnee, Seneca, Delaware, Ottawa, Pottawatomie, and Chippewa tribes ceded to the United States all Indian lands lying within the territory granted to them by the treaty of Greenville in 1795, except the district north of the Maumee River which had been ceded in 1808, and certain reservations within the territory for use as Indian lands, one of which comprised a track ten miles square at Wapakoneta, and one twenty-five miles square adjoining the Wapakoneta reservations along Hog Creek. In 1831 a sale of this land was negotiated with the Shawnees, and the following year all Indians were removed to Missouri.

Various European nations also held claims to the territory at different times. The first of those, Spain, based its interest in the land on the line of Demarcation established by Pope Alexander VI, which, in 1493, gave Spain title to all lands unoccupied by Christians west of the thirty-eighth meridian. Spanish claims were never advanced through occupancy, and in time the conflicting claims of France and England became paramount. The voyages of Jacques Cartier in 1535 and John and Sebastian Cabot in 1507, were the basis for French and English claims respectively. The entrance of missionaries and traders from France in the seventeenth century strengthened French title to the land. English claims were secured by the charters granted colonists in Virginia during the first quarter of the same century. French title to the land was relinquished in 1763 when Canada, together with the territory of which the present Allen County was then a part, was ceded to England at the close of the French and Indian wars.

At the close of the Revolutionary War, Virginia surrendered its claims secured through the charters granted by the English Crown, to the Congress of the United States, and the district was administered as a part of the Northwest Territory. In 1793, Hamilton County, administered at Fort Washington, was organized. This county included all territory lying between the Miami and Scioto rivers north to Lake Erie and Lake Huron. Four years later, following the Treaty of Greenville, Wayne County was organized. This county included all Indian territory north of the treaty line, and was administered from Detroit.

Allen County proper was laid out in 1820, from the Indian territory gained in the treaty of 1817. The county, as originally organized, included sixteen townships and was attached to Mercer County for judicial purpose with the county seat at St. Marys. The townships thus administered comprised Allen County until 1848 when an act of the state legislature established Auglaize County out of territory taken from Allen and Mercer counties. The southern townships of Clay, Duchouquet, Goshen, Molton, Pusheta, Union, Washington, and Wayne were at this time detached from Allen County. At the same time a strip one section wide was detached on the south of Shawnee Township, and a strip three sections wide was detached from the south of Amanda Township. To compensate for this loss of territory Richland and Monroe townships and the southern half of Sugar Creek and Jennings townships were detached from Putnam County and added to the north of Allen County. A strip one section wide, taken from Riley Township, also in Putnam County, was added to Richland Township. At this time a strip three miles wide and nine miles long was added in the west. This, with the exception of a two mile square which was annexed to Marion Township, was organized as Spencer Township.

No further additions to nor subtractions from the county have been made since 1848, although in 1857, Ottawa Township was formed from German, Bath, Perry, and Shawnee townships for the purpose of administrating the village of Lima. In 1917, shortly after America's entrance into the World War, the name of German Township was changed to American Township, a name which it still retains.

Immediately following the organization of Allen County the courts were held in connection with Mercer County, and none of the records were kept within the bounds of the county for several years. As nearly as can be ascertained the county was first administered from Hardin, which was at that time the county seat of Shelby County. Later the seat of government was moved to St. Marys, in Mercer County, where it remained for a short time before being removed to Allentown where the first court actually held in Allen County convened.

The first court held in Lima was an August 1831, in a log cabin belonging to James Daniels. The following year a log courthouse was constructed just south of the public square.

In 1840, a contract for a brick courthouse was let, and in 1842 the county took possession of the building which is located on the west side of public square. This building remained in use until 1884 when the present courthouse which stands at the corner of North Main and North Streets was erected.

The Commissioners' Journal for 1882 contains the record of a complaint by the county treasurer on the condition of the foundation of the courthouse. According to his statements the need of either a new courthouse or extensive repairs on the one then in use was imperative. He states that unless the foundation of the courthouse, especially that part under the safe, was strengthened before the frost was out of the ground his own life was in jeopardy and the records were in danger of being destroyed. Soon after this date bonds were issued for the construction of a new building.

This building, completed in 1884, has been in constant use since that time. In 1929, fire completely destroyed the west wing of the building. After the fire the section of the building that was destroyed was replaced with a modern, well-equipped wing with adequate space for the storage and use of the records of the offices located there.

Ohio counties were laid out to fit the needs of an agricultural society for the nineteenth century. The last Ohio county was created in 1851 and there have been no changes in boundaries for over half a century. The counties now range in population from 10,000 to 1,200,000. Approximately seventy of Ohio's eighty-eight counties may be considered rural. (Heiges, R.E., *The Office of Sheriff in the Rural Counties of Ohio*. Findlay, Ohio 1933, 52.) The average population is 30,000 but over half of the people live in eight large urban counties.

The county is a creation of the state for the execution of state policy and has such powers as the state confers on it. It has, however, had to provide an ever increasing number of local services similar to those rendered by municipalities and its legal statute is therefore changing. The county eventually may be relatively less the agent of the state and tend to approximate the municipal corporation in the character of its activities and its legal status. (Report of Governor's Commission, *The Reorganization of County Government in Ohio*, 1934, 3, 28-29.)

The board of county commissioners is the central feature of the structure of county government. The functions of this board touch either directly or indirectly every other branch and department. The board is the agency in whose name actions, for and against the county are brought. This board is empowered to determine certain policies for the conduct of county affairs such as adoption of the budget, establishment of services left optional by law, and the authorization of improvements. Thus, in a limited sense constitutes the legislative branch. The board also functions as a central administrative body although much of the administration, centered in other elective offices, is beyond its control. The county auditor was originally made secretary of the board and still functions as such in a majority of the counties. Later provisions of the law permitted the board to adopt its own clerk, thus removing this duty from the auditor. (*Ibid*., 58-59.)

There are three types of financial functions performed by county officers and employees: tax administration, handling of the fiscal affairs of the county, and a trusteeship of funds held for individuals in court procedure. The principal financial authorities are the board of commissioners, the auditor, and the treasurer. The commissioners levy taxes, appropriate funds, and authorize payments. The auditor's primary duties are the keeping of the accounts, the issuance of warrants, the valuation of real estate, and the preparation of the tax list. The treasurer collects taxes, receives and has custody of county moneys, and disburses upon warrant from the auditor. (*Ibid*., 71.)

There are three strictly clerical officers who work consists mainly of the preparation and custody of records: the recorder, the clerk of courts, and the judge of the probate court. All three have some part in the recording of documents and instruments affecting the title of property and of other documents presented for record. The last two have as their principal duty the keeping of court records; the clerk of courts serving both as clerk of the court of appeals and the common pleas court, and the probate court looking after its own records. (*Ibid*., 179.)

It is the duty of the recorder to copy, index, and file documents authorized to be recorded in his office. These consist almost entirely of chattel mortgages and instruments affecting the title to real estate. (*Ibid*., 180.) The system of recording is prescribed by statute. With the exception of a few urban counties recording is done by typewriter with considerable use of printed forms. The photographic method of copying is now in use in Clark, Cuyahoga, Hamilton, Lucas, Montgomery, and Summit counties.

The principal records of the clerk of courts are prescribed by statute. They include an appearance docket, an execution docket, a journal of the orders of the court, a complete record of case papers, a system of indexes, and the file of original papers. The clerk is responsible for a variety of non-judicial record work, of which the filing and indexing of the automobile bills of sales is the major item. At present the clerk acts as the agent of the state for the sale of hunting and fishing licenses and also issues auctioneers' and ferry licenses.

The probate judge is by statute the clerk of his own court, the Constitution permits the combination of the probate and common pleas courts in counties of less than 60,000 population. In this case the judge of common pleas become *ex officio* the clerk of the probate division and two separate offices are retained for keeping records. Such mergers now exist in three counties: Adams, Henry, and Wyandot. (*Ibid*., 182-83.)

Listed below, with amendments, are some notable provisions adopted at the convention of 1851 and 1912 which affected the organization of county government:

"Laws may be passed to secure to mechanics, artisans, laborers, subcontractors and material men there just dues by direct lien upon the property, upon which they have bestowed labor or for which they have furnished material." (Art. III, sec. 33. 1851.)

"All nominations for elective, state, district, county, and municipal offices shall be made at the direct primary election or by petition as provided by law . . . " (Art. V, sec. 7. 1912.)

"The general assembly shall provide by general law for the organization and government of counties, and may provide by general law alternative forms of county government. No alternative form shall become operative in any county until submitted to the electors thereof and approved by a majority of those voting . . . Municipalities and townships shall have authority with the consent of the county, to transfer to the county any of their powers or to revoke the transfer of any such power, under regulations provided by general law, but the rights of initiative and referendum shall be secured to every measure giving or withdrawing such consent." (Art. X, sec. 1, amendment adopted 1933.)

"Appointments and promotions in the civil service of the state, the several counties and cities, shall be made according to merit and fitness, to be ascertained, as far as practicable, by competitive examinations." (Art. XV, sec. 10. 1912)

"Elections for state and county officers shall be held on the first Tuesday after the first Monday in November in the even-numbered years." (Art. XVII, sec. 1, amendment adopted 1905."

The aim of the survey has been to make information available regarding the records which have accumulated over a period more than 130 years. Survey workers have not made a study of the functions of the county offices with a view toward recommending any reorganization of the county government but in the report of the Governor's Commission (*op. cit.*, 186-187.) recommendations were made bearing upon the records system as follows:

1. County Charters and optional forms of government should provide for a department of records and court service to take over the function of the recorder and clerk of courts, the non-judical record work of the probate court, and the functions of the sheriff as a court officer. (See also Heiges, *op. cit.*, 55-66.)

2. The issuance of licenses should be transferred from the clerk of courts to the department of finance.

3. Wider use should be made of the photographic process of recording in large counties.

4. Legislation should be adopted permitting the destruction of chattel mortgages and automotive bills of sale after they have ceased to have effect.

5. The requirements of the system of indexes of cases and the clerk's office should be eliminated from the code and only the index of pending suits and living judgments shall be required.

6. Provisions should be made in the rules of the common pleas court for service of process by mail and that method should be brought into general use. (See also Heiges, *op. cit.*, 60-61.)

Following the report of the governor's commission a new law (116 O.L. 132-33) was passed in 1933 permitting any county to adopt a charter or an alternative form of government, as provided in section 3 of Article X of the Constitution of Ohio, if it does not interfere with or restrict in any manner a charter which has been adopted by any municipal government. The electors may establish by charter provision a civil service commission or personnel department. In April 1935 (116 O.L. 134.) the legislature also provided that the electors of any county may established by charter provision a county department of health.

The legal development of the various county offices has been treated in a prefatory section proceeding the inventory of the records of each office.

In general, the records of Allen County are in good condition. In the majority of offices there are proper facilities for using the records and ample space for reasonable expansion. In the following paragraphs the facilities in each office are described separately.

Records of the county recorder are nearly all kept in two rooms on the second floor of the county courthouse. These records are all in excellent condition, the bound volumes being kept on steel roller shelves, and the unbound material in steel file cabinets. A few of the bound records are kept on wood roller shelves, and some of the outlawed chattel mortgages are in a tier of wood pigeon holes. There is room for expansion of the office for several years. A few of the old records are kept in an attic store room. These are in poor condition, but most of the material consists of records which have been transcribed. Accommodations for users of the recorder's office are good.

The office of the county engineer is located on the first floor of the courthouse, and includes three rooms in the northeast corner of the building. The ventilation of the room, as well as lighting, is good. Shelving is made of wood, and according to employees, there is ample room for expansion to other offices.

The office of the clerk of courts comprises three rooms on the second floor of the courthouse. The rooms are all well lighted and are well ventilated. Records in all of the rooms are clean and are in good condition. With the exception of the license bureau there is ample room for expansion for several years. In the license bureau, however, all of the available space has been utilized, and according to employees of the department, more space is needed. Records kept in this room consist of automobile bills of sale and license records. Shelving in this office consists of steel roller shelves and one steel counter which contain shelves. Steel file cabinets are used for all unbound records except those of active cases before the courts, which are kept in fiber cases during the action, and are transferred to the steel files after the cases are closed. There is a large table and two long counters for the accommodations of persons wishing to consult records.

The offices of the probate court are located on the second floor of the courthouse and consist of three rooms, two of which are used for housing records. There is good natural and artificial lighting in each of the rooms; the ventilation is good. The records are free from dust and soot. Wood roller shelves along three walls provide space for the bound volumes. Unbound records are kept in steel file cabinets. Accommodations for users are limited to counter space in the outer office. There is room for expansion for several years with present facilities, and ample space for the addition of new shelving and files.

The sheriff's office consists of two well lighted rooms on a second floor of the courthouse. Records are kept in but one of these. Steel file boxes are used for the unbound records. This room is slightly crowded with no room for expansion. Ventilation is good and it is free from dust and soot. Accommodations for users are limited.

The office of the county auditor includes three rooms on the second floor and two rooms directly below on the first floor of the courthouse. The records are in good condition and kept either on steel roller shelves or in steel file cabinets and drawers. While the rooms on the second floor are slightly crowded, there is ample room for expansion in the rooms on the first floor which are used for filing the active records. There is sufficient space for several users in each room. With the exception of one room on the second floor, the rooms are well lighted and ventilated. The records are in good condition, being clean and in good state of repair.

The office of the county treasurer includes three rooms on the second floor of the courthouse. These rooms are crowded. One of the rooms set aside for the treasurer is in use for the sales tax division. Shelving in use in this office is wooden. Unbound records are kept in steel files. Many of the records from the treasurer's office are kept in the auditor's office and some are stored in the attic storerooms.

The office of the county superintendent of schools consists of three rooms located on the second floor of the courthouse. Two of these rooms are used for filing records, one being well lighted and having good ventilation. The other is not much larger than a closet and contains steel shelving on which are kept all bound records of the office. Unbound records are kept in wood file cabinets located in the larger room. There is sufficient room for expansion.

The office of county recorder, although not unknown as early English institution for the registration of land titles, developed in colonial America where, due to the mobility of the restless pioneers, changes in land titles were frequent and some system was needed to protect purchasers against previous encumbrances. Public land registers, established in most of the colonies during the colonial period, continued by the states following independence, and provided a model of land registration for the territory of which the present state of Ohio was then a part. Thus the office of county recorder was established by an act of the Northwest Territory passed on August 1, 1795. This act, adopted from the Pennsylvania code, provided for the appointment by the governor of a recorder in each county whose principal duty was the recording of deeds. (Theodore Calvin Pease, *Laws of the Northwest Territory 1788- 1800*, Ill. State Bar Assn., Law Ser., Springfield, 1925, 1, 197-199.)

When Ohio entered the union in 1802 no constitutional provision was made for the continuation of the office, but the legislature during its first session passed an act providing for a recorder in each county to be appointed by the judge of the court of common pleas for a seven-year term. (1 O.L. 137.) The recorder continued to be an appointive officer until 1829, when, by an act of the legislature, he became elected for a three-year term. (27 O.L. 65.) The term remained at three years until the constitutional amendment of November 7, 1905, which provided for the election of all county officers in even numbered years. (*Ohio Const.* Art. XVIII, sec. 2.) The term of office was fixed at two years, and so continued until the amendment of 1933, which extended the term of the incumbent until January 1937 at which time the recorder, elected at the regular election in November 1936, should serve a four-year term. (115 O.L. 191.)

The first county recorder was directed by statute to record "all deeds, mortgages and conveyances of lands and tenements," lying within his county, and also all instruments and writings which were required by law to be recorded. (1 O.L. 137.) In 1818 he was directed to record all plats and maps of newly laid out villages and divisions or subdivisions of towns and villages. In 1835 he was permitted, when authorized by the county commissioners, to transcribe from the records of other counties all deeds, mortgages, and other instruments of writing for the sale or conveyance of lands, tenements, or hereditaments. (33 O.L. 8; 35 O.L. 10-11.)

Since that time many new duties have been added besides those of recording land titles. The present practice of recording powers of attorney began in 1831. (29 O.L. 346.) Successive acts in 1865, 1872, 1881, 1884, 1888, 1904, and 1923 added new duties in the recording of soldiers' discharges (62 O.L. 59.), copies of certificates of compliance authorizing companies not incorporated under the law of Ohio to transact business in the state, and certify copies of renewal as granted by such companies to their agents (69 O.L. 32.), limited partnership agreements (78 O.L. 248), stallion keepers liens (81 O.L. 179.), partition fence records (97 O.L. 140.), and federal tax liens (110 O.L. 252.) The recording of chattel mortgages and conditional sales, made compulsory in 1846 was made optional in 1878. (44 O.L. 61-62; 75 O.L. 519.) Although the act of 1935 provided for the filing of chattel mortgages with the recorder exclusively, such filings were not made mandatory. (G.C. sec. 8, 561.)

In the latter part of the nineteenth century an important extension of the method of recording land titles was provided by an act of the general assembly. The "Torrens System," as provided by the act of 1896 (92 O.L. 220.) was declared unconstitutional by the supreme court of Ohio as being repugnant to Sec. 16 of the bill of rights of the state constitution. (56 O.L. 575.) The present act, passed in 1913 (amended in 1913 and 1915), provides for the examination of land titles by the recorder and the issuance, if the title proved to be held in fee simple, of a certificate of title by the courts. The official certificate becomes the title of ownership and is indefeasible. However, in the event an interest is found in the land, after the issuance of the certificate, a claim is allowed to the legal claimant from a fund created for that purpose at the time of registration. (G.C. sec. 8, 572-34 - 8, 572-56; 106 O.L. 225; 115 O.L. 445-47.). This system, although adopted by a few counties has proved unpopular because of the difficulty of replacing the traditional complicated system.

The recorder, like other county officials, has been required to keep record of the business of his office. Although records were prescribed in earlier years, it was not until the middle of the nineteenth century that the legislature enacted measures prescribing the form and contents of such records, looking forward to some uniformity in land registration. Since 1850 the recorder has been required to keep a record of deeds in which is recorded all deeds, powers of attorney, and other instruments of writing for the unconditional sale of land, tenements or hereditaments. (48 O.L. 64.) The same year saw the beginning of a record of mortgages in which was recorded all mortgages, powers of attorney, and other instruments of writing by which land, tenements or hereditaments "shall or may be mortgaged" or otherwise conditionally sold; and a record of plats in which was to be recorded all plats and maps of town lots and of subdivisions thereof, and of other divisions or surveyed lands, in like regular succession according to the priority of their presentation. (480 O.L. 64.) Since 1851 the recorder has been required to keep a separate record of mortgages denominated as "Record of Deeds" and "Record of

Mortgages." (49 O.L. 103.) Ten years later saw the beginning of a separate record of leases in which the recorder was, and is, required to record all leases and powers of attorney for the execution of leases. (61 O.L. 55.) The present practices of keeping a daily register of deeds and a daily register of mortgages had its beginning in 1896. In this record are recorded in alphabetical order the names of the grantors of all deeds and mortgages affecting real estate. (92 O.L. 268.)

The present system of indexing, although indexes had been prepared in earlier years, had its beginning in 1851 and took practically its present form in 1896. (49 O.L. 103; 92 O.L. 268; 102 O.L. 277.) At present the recorder, at the beginning of each day's business, is required to make and keep up a general alphabetical index, direct and reverse of all names of both parties of all instruments recorded by him. The indexes show the kind of instrument, the date, the range, township and section, the survey number and the number of acres, or the lot and sublot numbers and the part thereof, of each tract or lot of land described in any such instrument of writing; the name of each grantor is entered in the direct index under the appropriate letter followed on the same line by the name of the grantee. The name of each grantee is entered in the reverse index under the appropriate letter followed on the same line by the name of the grantor. (G.C. sec. 2, 764.)

Since 1859 the county commissioners have been authorized to provide sectional indexes to the records of all real estate in the county, beginning with some designated year and continuing through a period of years as may be specified. (G.C. sec. 2, 766; 64 O.L.256; 76 O.L. 49; 102 O.L. 277.)

The present duties of the recorder do not differ, in the main, from those prescribed in the middle of the nineteenth century. His records, in large bulky volumes, are open to the inspection of the public, and are transferred to his successor.

Deeds

1. REGISTER OF CONVEYANCES
1877-1896. 12 Vols.

A record listing names of grantors and grantees, number of deed, mortgage or other conveyance, consideration, and date. Alphabetical index in front of each volume. Handwritten. Volumes average 222 pages. 16 x 11 x 1.25. County courthouse, room 400A.

2. REGISTER OF DEEDS
1896—. 17 vols.

A daily register of deeds, deed numbers, names of grantor and grantee, dates and description of property. Chronologically arranged. Handwritten. Volumes average 450 pages. 14 x 12 x 3.5. County courthouse.

1896-1928, 14 volumes, room 400A.
1929—, 3 volumes room, 204.

3. RECORD OF DEEDS
1831—. 257 vols.

A record of all deeds, warranty deeds, quit-claim deeds, deeds with dower, administrator's or executor's deeds, sheriff's deeds, and corporation deeds. Indexed by separate volumes, see entry 4. 1831-1925, handwritten; 1925—, typed. Volumes average 625 pages. 18 x 12 x 3.5. County courthouse, north room 204.

4. GENERAL INDEX TO DEEDS
1831—. 22 Vols.

A record listing names that grantor and grantee of each deed, name of instrument, number of instrument, volume number and page where recorded. Handwritten. Volumes average 600 pages. 18 x 12 x 3.5. County courthouse, north room 204.

Leases

5. LEASES AND AGREEMENTS
1871—. 41 vols.

Written agreements and land contracts. Alphabetically index in front of each volume. 1871-1916, handwritten; 1906—, typed. Volumes average 600 pages. 18 x 12 x 3.5. County courthouse, north room 204.

6. DAILY REGISTER OF LEASES, ALLEN COUNTY
1898—. 2 vols.

A daily record listing names of grantor and grantee, date and number of acres called for in each lease. Alphabetically arranged as to names of grantors and grantees. Handwritten. Volumes average 600 pages. 14 x 12 x 3.5. County courthouse.

1898-1925, 1 volume, north room 204.
1926—, 1 volume, room 204.

Mortgages

7. RECORD OF MORTGAGES
1831—. 215 vols.

A record of mortgages, listing names of grantor and grantee, description of property, number of mortgage, date of mortgage, and date of recording for each entry. Indexed by separate volumes, see entry 8. 1831-1900, handwritten; 1900-1920, handwritten on printed forms; 1930—, typed. Volumes average 600 pages. 18 x 12 x 3.5. County courthouse, north room 204.

8. GENERAL INDEX OF MORTGAGES
1854—. 20 vols.

An alphabetically index of mortgagors and mortgagees, grantors and grantees, listing date of filing and number of each instrument, volume and page of the record. Handwritten. Volumes average 600 pages. 18 x 12 x 3.5. County courthouse.

1854-1870, 2 volumes, room 204.
1854—, 18 volumes, north room 204.

9. REGISTER OF MORTGAGES
1896—. 17 vols.

A daily register of mortgages listing name of grantor and grantee, mortgage number, amount, and date. Chronologically arranged. Handwritten. Volumes average 400 pages. 14 x 12 x 3. County courthouse.

1896-1928, 14 volumes room 400A
1929—, 3 volumes room 204.

10. RELEASE OF MORTGAGE RECORD
1891—. 8 vols.

A record of release of mortgages. Alphabetically index in front of each volume.

1891-1906, handwritten; 1905—, typed. Volumes average 600 pages. 18 x 12 x 3.5. County courthouse, north room 204.

11. CANCELLATION OF MORTGAGES
1905—, 3 vols.

A daily record of cancellation of mortgages, listing name of grantor and grantee, date, and mortgage number. Chronologically arranged. Handwritten. Volumes average 600 pages. 18 x 12 x 3.5. County courthouse.

1905-1926, 2 volumes, north room 204.
1926—, 1 volume, room 204.

12. MORTGAGE DEEDS
1900-1922. 26 pigeon holes.

Cancelled mortgages. Alphabetically arranged. 10 x 10 x 5. County courthouse, north room 204.

13. COURT RELEASES
No date. 1 file box.

This box contains court releases. Papers not open to public inspection. No index. 10 x 10 x 5. County courthouse, room 204.

14. CHATTEL MORTGAGES
1878—, 2 vols.

A regulation record of chattel mortgages. Alphabetical index in front of each volume. 1878-1915, handwritten on printed forms; 1915—, typed. Volumes average 600 pages. 18 x 12 x 3.5. County courthouse, room 204.

15. CHATTEL MORTGAGES
1848—. 101 file boxes, 13 pigeon holes.

Regulation chattel mortgages. Older ones 1848-1904; newer form 1930—. The files are dated and indexed by separate volumes, see entry 16. 10 x 10 x 5. County courthouse.

1848-1904, 13 pigeon holes, north room 204.
1930—, 101 file boxes, room 204.

16. INDEX TO CHATTEL MORTGAGES

1878—. 31 vols.

A general index to chattel mortgages, listing names of grantor and grantee, dates, amounts, and file box number. Handwritten. Volumes average 600 pages. 18 x 12 x 3.5. County courthouse.

1878-1911, 10 volumes, north room 204.

1912—, 21 volumes, room 204.

Liens

17. MECHANICS' LIENS

1883—. 7 vols. (— 1883, 1891-1898, missing.)

A record containing ordinary mechanic's liens, listing names and dates. Alphabetical index in front of each volume. 1883-1913, handwritten; 1913—, typed. Volumes average 600 pages. 18 x 12 x 3.5. County courthouse, north room 204.

18. RECORD OF LIENS, LEASES, TRUSTS, AND EXCEPTIONAL ESTATES

1916—. 1 vol.

A record of liens, trust, leases, and exceptional estates. Alphabetical index in front of volume. Handwritten. 600 pages. 14 x 12 x 3.5. County courthouse, room 204.

19. TAX PAYMENT LIEN

1926-1930. 1 vol.

Authorization of banks to pay taxes on certain properties. Alphabetical index in front of volume. Typed. 600 pages. 18 x 12 x 3.5. County courthouse, north room 204.

20. INDEX OF LIEN NOTICES AND DISCHARGES

1930—. 1 vol.

A description of the property, names of parties, dates, and amounts of surety. Handwritten. 600 pages. 18 x 12 x 3.5. County courthouse, room 204.

21. FEDERAL TAX LIEN INDEX

1925. 1 vol.

An index listing names of taxpayers, residence, and amount. Handwritten. 250 pages. 14 x 14 x 1.5. County courthouse, room 204.

22. SUBCONTRACTORS' LIEN RECORD
1888-1911. 1 vol.

A contractor's record of liens. Alphabetically arranged as to names of contractors. Handwritten. 250 pages. 14 x 12 x 1.5. County courthouse, room 204.

23. RECORDER'S PERSONAL TAX LIEN RECORD
1932-1934. 1 vol.

A personal tax record. No index. Handwritten. 150 pages. 12 x 8 x 1. County courthouse, room 204.

24. EXCISE AND FRANCHISE TAX LIEN, AN INDEX TO CORPORATION RECORD
1931—. 1 vol.

A record listing name of taxpayer, residence, and amount. Handwritten. 250 pages. 14 x 14 x 1.5. County courthouse, room 204.

Torrens Department

25. REGISTERED LAND, INDEX OF OWNER
1915. 1 vol.

A record giving each owner's name, description, and location of lands. Numerical index. Handwritten. 600 pages. 18 x 12 x 3.5. County courthouse, room 204.

26. REGISTERED LANDS, INDEX OF LIENS AND LESSER ESTATES
1 vol.

A blank volume. 600 pages. 18 x 12 x 3.5. County courthouse, room 204.

27. REGISTERED LANDS, RECEPTION BOOK
1915. 1 vol.

A record showing daily receipts of documents pertaining to the registered lands. Lists kind of document, description of land, and name of owner. No index. Handwritten. 600 pages. 18 x 12 x . 35. County courthouse, room 204.

28. REGISTERED LAND, REGISTER OF TITLE
1916. 1 vol.

This record gives original certificate and transfer certificate of title to the land. Numerical index. Typed. 600 pages. 18 x 12 x 3.5. County courthouse, room 204.

29. REGISTERED LANDS, SURVEY
No date. 1 vol.
Blank volume. Place for alphabetical index in front of volume. 600 pages. 18 x 12 x 3.5. County courthouse, room 204.

Abstract Division

30. ABSTRACT Of ALLEN COUNTY
1834-1880. 16 VOLS.
An abstract record of titles of Allen County. Alphabetical index in front of each volume. Handwritten. Volumes average 600 pages. 18 x 12 x 3.5. County courthouse, north room 204.

31. ABSTRACTS
1835—. 48 vols.
A complete record of abstracts listed under each taxing district. Alphabetical index on printed form on end of shelf. Handwritten. Volumes average 600 pages. 18 x 12 x 3.5. County courthouse, north room 204.

32. ABSTRACT RECORD, ALLEN COUNTY, OHIO
1835-1908. 5 vols.
A record of mortgages listing name of grantor, grantee, date of mortgage and date of recording. No index. Handwritten. Volumes average 600 pages. 18 x 12 x 3.5. County courthouse, north room 204.

33. LIMA ABSTRACT RECORD
1864-1932 2 vols.
A record of deeds and mortgages of lots in the city of Lima, listing names, dates, amounts, and giving description of each property. No index. Handwritten. Volumes average 600 pages. 18 x x12 x 3.5. County courthouse, north room 204.

Corporations

34. RECORD OF INCORPORATED SOCIETIES, NO. 2
1872-1902. 1 vol.
A record of Articles of Incorporation for various societies, listing names, addresses, and other information about the societies. Alphabetical index in front of volume.

Handwritten. 450 pages. 17 x 12 x 3. County courthouse, north room 204.

35. CORPORATION RECORD
1931-1933. 1 VOL.

A notice of payment of taxation and excise record. Alphabetical index in front of volume; also indexed by separate volume. See entry 24. Typed on printed forms. 600 pages. 18 x 12 x 3.5. County courthouse, room 204.

36. LIMITED PARTNERSHIP RECORD
1884-1928. 1 vol.

A record of partnership agreements, names, addresses, nature of partnership. Alphabetical index in front of volume. There are printed forms in the volume, but they were not used and the information is handwritten. 300 pages. 16 x 12 x 2. County courthouse, north room 204.

37. INDIVIDUAL AND PARTNERSHIP TRADER'S RECORD
1884-1885. 1 vol.

A record listing names of partners, occupation, and location of business. Alphabetical index in front of volume. Handwritten on printed forms. 600 pages. 18 x 12 x 3.5. County courthouse, north room 204.

Record of Certificates, Licenses, and Grants of Authority

38. INSURANCE CERTIFICATE
1916—. 14 file boxes, 6 pigeon holes.

These are insurance certificates dating from 1916 to 1921, and 1930 to date. Filed chronologically. Indexed by separate volumes, see entry 39. 10 x 10 x 5. County courthouse.

1916-1921, 6 pigeon holes. North room 204.
1930—, 14 file boxes. Room 204.

39. INDEX TO INSURANCE CERTIFICATE RECORD
6 vols.

A record of insurance certificates filed, Listing name of county, state where incorporated, assets, liabilities, date, and file box number. Handwritten. Volumes average 300 pages. 16 x 12 x 2. County courthouse.

1921, 4 volumes. Room 400A.
1922—, Two volumes. North room 204.

40. INSURANCE COMPLIANCE CERTIFICATE

1927-1934. Three pigeon holes.

Recorded insurance compliance certificates. Indexed by separate volumes, see entry 41. County courthouse, north room 204.

41. INSURANCE COMPLIANCE RECORD

1871—. 4 vols.

Index and register of insurance compliance certificates filed, listing name of county, state where incorporated, assets, liabilities, and date. Chronologically arranged. Handwritten. Volumes average 300 pages. 16 x 12 x 2. County courthouse.

1871-1921, 3 volumes. Room 400A.
1925—, 1 volume. North room 204.

42. CERTIFIED COPIES OF AGENTS' LICENSES

1927-1934. 5 pigeon holes.

Certified copies of agents' licenses of various insurance companies. No index. 10 x 10 x 5. County courthouse. North room 204.

43. POWER OF ATTORNEY'S RECORD

1872—. 2 vols.

These are regulation forms of power of attorney, listing names, dates, addresses, etc. Alphabetical index in front of each volume. 1877-1907, handwritten; 1908—, typed. Volumes average 600 pages. 18 x 12 x 3.5. County courthouse. North room 204.

44. RECORD OF AUTHORITY TO PAY TAXES

1894-1898. 1 vol.

A record of names of persons authorized to pay taxes, dates, description of each property, amount of tax, and owner's name. Alphabetical index in front of volume. Handwritten on printed forms. 600 pages. 18 x 12 x 3.5. County courthouse. North room 204.

Miscellaneous

45. RECORD OF ENTRIES OF ALLEN COUNTY
1825-1847. 1 vol.

A record of original entries of Allen County. Lists name of settler, location of land, date of entry, and farmer's resident when known. (There are two copies.) Indexed as to township, section, and range numbers. Handwritten. Volumes average 150 pages. 16 x 12 x 1.5. County courthouse. North room 204.

46. RECORD OF NOTICE OF INTENTION TO SELL AND TRANSFER STOCK OF GOODS
1889. 1 vol.

A record of notices of intention to transfer stock of goods, listing names, dates, and kinds of goods. Alphabetical index in front of volume. Handwritten. 250 pages. 14 x 12 x 1.5. County courthouse. Room 204.

47. FENCE RECORD NO. 1
1904-1934. 1 vol.

A record of agreements for establishment of line fences, listing names, dates, locations, etc. Alphabetical index in front of volume. Handwritten and typed. 600pages. 18 x 12 x 3.5. County courthouse. Room 204.

48. RECORD OF SOLDIERS' DISCHARGES
1861—. 6 vols.

A record of each soldiers' and sailors' official discharge, listing oath of identity, enlistment record, and discharge. Alphabetical index in front of each volume. Handwritten on printed forms. 5 volumes average 600 pages. 18 x 12 x 3.5; 1 volume has 200 pages. 14 x 8 x 1. County courthouse. Room 204.

49. EX-OFFICIO SERVICE, ALLEN COUNTY,
1 vol.

A blank volume. 200 pages. 16 x 12 x 1. County courthouse. North room 204.

50. MISCELLANEOUS

No date. 40 file boxes.

These boxes contain deeds, mortgages, liens and other legal documents held in trust by the recorder. Index on front of each file box. 10 x 10 x 5. County courthouse. Room 204.

51. MISCELLANEOUS RECORDS

1906-1935. 2 vols.

A record of contracts of various kinds, divorcements, bills of sale, etc. Alphabetical index in front of each volume. 1906-1927, handwritten; 1927-1935, typed. Volumes average 600 pages. 18 x 12 x 3.5. County courthouse. North room 204.

Maps and Plat Books

52. MAP OF ALLEN COUNTY

1925. 1 map.

A political map of Allen County showing names of owners of farms, the position of roads, rivers, and villages. Walter C. Ferguson, Lima, Ohio, publisher. Printed and mounted. No scale. 58 x 40. County courthouse. North room 204.

53. TOWNSHIP MAPS

1931. 12 maps.

Political maps showing farms according to names of owners; also roads, rivers and villages. Drafting supervised by John E. Breese, C.E., Gamble and Gordon, Lima, Ohio, publishers. Printed. No scale. 11 maps average 27 x 30; 1 map is 36 x 29. County courthouse. Room 204, in map case.

54. MAP OF LIMA

1908. 1 map.

A political and communications map of Lima, showing lot numbers, streets, stream railways, electric railways, section lines, half section lines, and range numbers. S. W. Funk, C.E., Lima, Ohio, publisher. Printed and framed. Scale, 1 inch equals 500 feet. 36 x 40. County courthouse. North room 204.

55. MAP OF LIMA, OHIO, AND VICINITY

1930. 1 map.

A political map of Lima, Ohio, showing lot numbers and streets. It has an index to out lots on the map. C.R. Gordon and N.F. Shook, publishers. Printed and mounted. No scale. 54 x 60. County courthouse. North room 204.

56. VILLAGE MAPS

1914. 7 maps.

Political maps of villages showing lot numbers and streets. John E. Breese, C.E., Lima, Ohio, publisher. Printed. Scales, 1 inch equals 100 feet, 150 feet, or 200 feet. Sizes average, 27 x 42. County courthouse. North room 204, in map case.

57. PLAT BOOKS

1850—. 12 vols.

A plat and description of the land, listing engineer's, clerk's, and auditor's certification, dates of transfer and recording. Alphabetical index in front of each volume. Handwritten. Volumes average 400 pages. 24 x 19 x 3. County courthouse. Room 204.

58. OLD AND NEW LOT NUMBERS, CITY AND TOWNS, ALLEN COUNTY

1831-1906. 2 vols.

Records of lot numbers in Lima and villages of Allen County, with dates of laying out additions, and name of surveyor. States which plat book contains plat of various subdivisions. (One is copy of the older book.) Alphabetical index in front of volume. Handwritten. Volumes average 200 pages. 14 x 8 x 1.5. County courthouse. North room 204.

The local governmental system for the Northwest Territory comprising present state of Ohio, established the office of county commissioners. This office, created by the territorial act of 1792, consisted of two appointive commissioners who were directed to compile a tax list, levy taxes for the county, and to draft plans for, and supervise the construction of a "courthouse, pillory whipping post, and several stocks." (Pease, *op. cit.*, 78.)

The governmental system established in 1803, under the first constitution of Ohio, made no provisions for the office and its existence is due entirely to statutory enactment. By an act of the legislature passed in 1804, the territorial office was recreated and was to be composed of three members elected for a three-year term. (2 O.L. 150.) Seven years later the commissioners were made a corporate body invested with the power to sue and to be sued. They were required to keep a record of their proceedings; to assess taxes for the support of the county; appoint a county treasurer; and to supervise the construction of bridges. (8 O.L. 358.) They were paid at a per diem rate. Moreover, during the same period they were given the task of constructing courthouses, jails, and offices for the clerk of courts, court of common pleas, the sheriff, the auditor, and the treasurer. (2 O.L. 156-157; 29 O.L. 315.) Of these earlier duties the commissioners retain all but one; that of appointing a county treasurer. However, since 1831 they have been authorized to examine and compare the accounts of the county treasurer and county auditor and to examine the conditions of county finances.

Besides the duties regarding construction and finance, the commissioners were given the task of constructing local highways when so authorized by the legislature. During the first thirty years of Ohio history the duties of the commissioners in this respect were local in nature. But as the system of road construction expanded they were given the additional duty of converting free turnpikes into state roads. (44 O.L. 74.) During the forties and fifties private companies were authorized by the legislature to construct plank roads. (44 O.L. 126-127.) When, in 1857, these companies were caught up in the stringency of a financial depression, the county commissioners were authorized to purchase their holdings. If such a transaction were made, the transfer signed by the president of the company was to be deposited with a county auditor. (54 O.L. 198.) In the seventies the commissioners, although earlier subjected to regulatory measures by the legislature, were prohibited from levying taxes for roads to exceed three mills on the dollar on the taxable property in the county. (69 O.L. 111.) Later, in 1887, they were authorized to levy taxes not to exceed five mills on the dollar on all taxable property in the county for the maintenance and upkeep of roads which had been damaged by excessive wear or were damaged from other causes. (G.C. sec. 7, 419.)

With the development of modern means of transportation, scientific principles were applied to road construction and maintenance. Although the county surveyor, now the county engineer, had in earlier years furnished the commissioners with estimates for bridge construction, it was not until the later part of the nineteenth century that they were authorized to utilize his scientific knowledge in road construction. (78 O.L. 285; O.L. 245-247.) At the opening of the present century the surveyor was directed to appoint a maintenance engineer, with the consent of the commissioners, to supervise repair of improved roads in the county. (108 O.L. pt. 1, 497.)

Although the county commissioners have never been closely associated with the administration of criminal justice, their earlier duties regarding the construction of county jails qualified them, in the early period, for additional duties in this respect. During the middle of the nineteenth century the commissioners of Cuyahoga and Hamilton counties were authorized to employ persons confined in county jails on construction work. (37 O.L. 54.) While this provision was repealed by the criminal code, adopted in 1853, other earlier functions applicable to all counties were continued. Since 1843 the commissioners have provided equipment and fixtures for places of incarceration, food, and clothing for prisoners; and appointed a jail physician. (41 O.L. 74; 87 O.L. 186.) Since 1869 they have been authorized to offer a reward for the detection or apprehension of any person charged with a felony in the county. Moreover, since 1929, the commissioners, in any county where there is no workhouse, may, under certain conditions, release or parole an indigent person confined in jail. (66 O.L. 287; 113 O.L. 123.) With the extension of modern crime into the rural areas, in the form of small-town bank robbing, the commissioners were given the duty of furnishing motorcycles to the sheriff and his deputies in an attempt to compete with the high powered equipment as used by modern gangs. One of the latest functions, in this respect, is the contracting with radio stations for the broadcasting of descriptions of fleeing criminals. (G.C. sec. 13, 431-1.)

Besides providing for those who have violated the laws of the county, the commissioners were given the duty of caring for persons, who, because of poverty, physical or mental defects, became a public charge. Since 1814 they have established and maintained "poor houses." (12 O.L. 298.) Since 1913 they have been authorized, in any county containing a city which has an infirmary, to contract with the director of public safety for the care of the county's indigent. (G.C. sec. 2, 419-1.)

In 1933 the commissioners were designated as a board to administer the state law providing aid for the aged. (115 O.L. pt. 2, 431-439.) Two years later, in 1935, the commissioners were authorized to provide non-institutional support, care, assistance, or relief for the county's indigent and were authorized to establish a suitable agency or office for such purposes. (116 O.L. 134.) Since 1908 the commissioners have been authorized to issue warrants for the relief of the blind in the sum of four hundred dollars per year. (G.C. sec. 2, 969.)

In addition to furnishing financial aid to the civilian population the commissioners were authorized (1886) to levy a tax for the relief of indigent soldiers, sailors or marines of the Civil War, or if such veterans were deceased, for the dependents. (83 O.L. 232.) In 1919 the provisions of the original act were amended to include all veterans. (108 O.L. pt. 1, 633.) The commissioners were authorized also, in 1884, to defray the funeral expenses of any honorable discharged soldier, sailor or marine who died indigent. Ten years later the provision of the act were extended to include the mother, wife or widow, of any soldier sailor or marine or any war nurse. (90 O.L. 177.)

The humanitarian duty of caring for the county's children was delegated to the county commissioners. Since 1824 they have been authorized to establish and maintain children's homes. At the beginning of the present century, when the treatment of children was undergoing a remarkable change, they were authorized to place dependent and neglected children in private homes or institutions where they would receive food, clothing, medical and dental treatment. (109 O.L. 533.) The development of the juvenile court system added new responsibilities. In order to completely segregate juvenile offenders from regular criminal courts, the commissioners were authorized to provide a separate building to be known as the "juvenile court."

The commissioners, by the authority conferred upon them to construct public buildings, were giving duties regarding educational advancements. Since 1871 they have been authorized to accept bequests for the construction of county libraries, and since 1913 to issue bonds, after submitting such questions to the voters, for the construction of libraries, or to contract with existing libraries for the use of the people in the county. (G.C. sec. 2, 454; 2, 134-1; 110 O.L. 242.) Moreover, during the same period, they were authorized to provide and maintain civic centers in the county and to employ an expert director to supervise and administer them. (G.C. sec. 2, 457-4.)

Other duties not closely related to the original duties of the commissioners have been added from decade to decade. For example, in 1850 they were authorized to subscribe for one leading newspaper of each political party in the county and cause them to be bound and deposited with the county auditor as public archives. (48 O.L. 65.) An amendment to the original act, passed in 1923, provided for the preservation of such newspapers for a period of ten years, after which they may be removed to the Ohio State Archaeological and Historical Society. (101 O.L. 4.) Besides this, they have been authorized to promote historical research by appropriating annually a sum not to exceed one hundred dollars to defray the expense of compiling and publishing historical data for historical societies not incorporated for profit. (G.C. sec 2, 457-1.)

During the early years of the twentieth century the commissioners were given the duty for providing facilities for county sanitation, which, in previous years had been sadly neglected. In 1917 they were authorized to lay out, establish and maintain one or more sewer districts within the county, and to employ a sanitary engineer to aid them in the performance of their duties. In counties having a population exceeding 100,000 the commissioners were authorized to create and maintain a sanitary engineering department. Since 1917 no sewer or sewerage treatment works may be constructed outside of any incorporated municipality by any person, persons, firms or corporations until the plans have been approved by the commissioners. (G.C. sec. 102-1; 107 O.L. 440.)

Then too, during the same period the commissioners were authorized to provide facilities for the treatment of tuberculosis. In 1913 they were empowered to appoint one or more visiting nurse to visit homes or places wherein there was a case of tuberculosis, and since 1917 have been authorized to establish tuberculosis dispensaries and provide by tax levies necessary funds for their establishment and maintenance. (G.C. sec. 3, 153; 153-5.) Meantime they were authorized to cooperate with the commissioners of other counties for the establishment of a district tubercular hospital. (100 O.L. 87.) Ten years later the commissioners in any county having more than 50,000 population, with the consent of the state department of health, were authorized to provide the necessary funds for the purchase or lease of a site and the erection and equipment or the lease and equipment of the necessary buildings thereon for the operation and maintenance of the county hospital for the treatment of persons suffering from tuberculosis. (108 O.L. pt. 1253; 109 O.L. 212; G.C. sec. 3, 148-1.) The management and control of such a hospital was vested in the commissioners.

Finally the county commissioners have acted in a supervisory capacity over other county officials. Since the middle of the nineteenth century they have been authorized to compare the annual reports and statements made to them by the prosecuting attorney, the clerk of courts, the sheriff, and the treasurer; take measures to rectify errors, correct discrepancies, and record in the journal the results of such examinations. (G.C. sec. 2, 504; R.S. 886; 48 O.L. 66.) Such reports were filed with the county auditor who acts as secretary to the commissioners and has custody of their official acts and proceedings. Moreover in the later part of the same century the commissioners were given their present-day duty of visiting and reporting on the sanitary conditions and the treatment of inmates in hospitals, detention homes, private asylums or any other institution exercising a reformatory or correctional influence over individuals. These reports, filed with the county prosecutor, are open to the inspection and examination of the public. (G.C. sec. 2, 498; 92 O.L. 212.)

The county commissioners offers a typical example of an office, which designed primarily for an agricultural society, has expanded to meet the needs and requirements of modern society. At present the commissioners are elected for a four-year term. (108 O.L. pt. 2, 1,300.)

Journals, Dockets and Reports

59. COMMISSIONERS' JOURNAL

1831—. 43 vols. (1879-1883, missing.)

A record of meetings and official proceedings of the commissioners. Indexed by separate volume, see entry 61. 1831-1908, handwritten; 1908—, typed. Volumes average 600 pages. 18 x 12 x 2. County courthouse.

1831-1879, 1883-1894, 1900-1902, 27 volumes. Room 101A.

1894-1900, 1915—, 5 volumes. Room 101.

60. COMMISSIONER'S JOURNAL

1925—. 1 vol. (— 1925, missing.)

A record of county home affairs. Indexed by separate volume, see entry 61. Typed. 600pages. 18 x 12 x 2. County courthouse. Room 101.

61. INDEX TO COMMISSIONERS' JOURNAL

1834—. 19 vols.

Index to various journals kept by county commissioners. Handwritten. 600 pages. 18 x 12 x 2.

1834-1898, 1909- 1914, 6 volumes. Room 202.

1896-1907, 5 volumes. Room 400B.

1913—, 8 volumes. Room 101.

62. COMMISSIONERS' DOCKET

1875-1883. 4 vols. (— 1875, missing.)

A record of proceedings of the board of county commissioner. No index. Handwritten. Volumes average 250 pages. 16 x 12 x 2. County courthouse. Room 202.

63. CLASSIFICATION BLOTTER FROM WHICH TO TAKE COMMISSIONERS' ANNUAL REPORT

1908-1915. 9 vols. (1909, 1912, 1914, missing.)

A record listing amounts of allotments, to whom paid, remarks, and miscellaneous business. Chronological index. Handwritten. Volumes average 100 pages. 18 x 12 x 1. County courthouse.

1905-1907, 2 volumes. Room 202.

1908-1911, 3 volumes. Room 101.

1913-1915, 4 volumes. Room 400B.

64. COMMISSIONERS' RECORD

1832-1860. 1 vol.

A record of oaths of justice of the peace. Alphabetical index in front of volume. Handwritten. 150 pages. 14 x 8 x 1. County courthouse. Room 202.

65. REPORTS

1929-1933. 1 file box.

Miscellaneous reports. Cardex system. 16 x 11 x 5. County courthouse. Room 101.

66. REPORTS, VARIOUS OFFICERS

1928-1933. 1 file box.

Filed reports of the various county officers. Cardex system. 16 x 11 x 5. County courthouse. Room 101.

67. DOG WARDEN'S REPORTS

1929—. 1 file box.

Reports made by the county dog warden. Cardex system. 16 x 11 x 5. County courthouse. Room 101.

68. SHEEP CLAIMS

1920—. 1 file box.

A record of claims made for loss of sheep by dogs. Cardex system. 16 x 11 x 5. County courthouse. Room 101.

Bridge, Ditch, Road and Sewer Records

69. COUNTY ROADS
1920—. 1 file box.
A record of cost and repair of county roads. Handwritten. 16 x 11 x 5. County courthouse. Room 101.

70. COMMISSIONERS' RECORDS
1920—, 27 file boxes.
Original papers relative to roads, bridges, and ditches, listed by townships. 17 x 10 x 2; 17 x 11.5 x 5; 23 x 15 x 12. County courthouse. Room 101.

71. I. C. H. LITIGATION MISCELLANEOUS
1920—. 1 file box.
Litigation and other miscellaneous records pertaining to improved highways. Cardex system. 16 x 11 x 5. County courthouse. Room 101.

72. COMMISSIONERS' RECORD OF ROADS
1834-1846. 1 vol. (— 1834, missing.)
A record of surveys of roads and Allen County. No index. Handwritten. 150 pages. 14 x 12 x 1. County courthouse. Room 202.

73. DAY BOOKS
1880-1893. 2 vols.
A record of county road funds listing receipts and expenditures. Alphabetical index of townships in front of volume. Handwritten. Volumes average 450 pages. 15 x 11 x 2. County courthouse. Room 400B.

74. COUNTY ROADS INSIDE OF CITY LIMITS AND VILLAGES
1920—. 1 file box.
A record of repairs, estimates, etc., of county roads inside city and villages. Cardex system. 16 x 11 x 5. County courthouse. Room 101.

75. I. C. H. ROADS COMPLETED
1920—. 2 file boxes.
A record of improved highways which have been completed. Cardex system. 16 x 11 x 5. Room 101.

76. WESTWOOD STREETS

1920—. 2 file boxes.

Records pertaining to Westwood streets completed and Westwood street petitions. Cardex system. 16 x 11 x 5. County courthouse. Room 101.

77. COMMISSIONERS' JOURNAL, SANITARY SEWER

1924-1933. 1 vol.

A record of proceedings with Westwood and Lost Creek sewage districts, listing boundaries and allowances. Indexed by separate volume. Typed. 600 pages. 18 x 12 x 2. County courthouse. Room 101.

78. MISCELLANEOUS SEWER DISTRICTS

1926—. 1 file box.

This contains miscellaneous records pertaining to sewer construction and repairs. Cardex system. 16 x 11 x 5. County courthouse. Room 101.

County Institutions and Relief Records

79. BLIND PENSIONS

1920—. 1 file box.

A record listing names of beneficiaries, dates, and amounts of blind pensions. Cardex system. 16 x 11 x 5. County courthouse. Room 101.

80. T.B. HOSPITAL - SPRINGBROOK PET. SEWER

1920—. 1 file box.

Various records pertaining to tuberculosis hospital. Also records of Springbrook sewer. Cardex system. 16 x 11 x 5. County courthouse. Room 101.

81. RECEIPTS AND EXPENDITURES

1928—. 1 vol.

A record of amounts received and paid for maintenance of the county infirmary, listing dates, amounts, and from what fund taken. No index. Handwritten. 250 pages. 17 x 15 x 1.5. Infirmary office.

82. REGISTER

1924—. 1 vol.

A record of the names and salaries of the employees of the county infirmary. Alphabetical index in front of volume. Handwritten. 288 pages. 14 x 9 x 1.5. Infirmary office.

Miscellaneous

83. BILLS OF SALE

1920—. 1 file box.

Miscellaneous bills of sale. Cardex system. 16 x 11 x 5. County courthouse. Room 101.

84. PAROLES AND REPOSSESSIONS

1920—. 1 file box.

Documents pertaining to paroles and repossessions. Cardex system. 16 x 11 x 5. County courthouse. Room 101.

85. RESOLUTIONS

1934. 1 file box.

The file box contains resolutions of the county commissioners. Cardex system. 16 x 11 x 5. County courthouse. Room 101.

86. TRANSFERS AND APPROPRIATIONS

1926-1933. 2 file boxes.

A record of transfers and appropriations of various county funds. Cardex system. 16 x 11 x 5. County courthouse. Room 101.

Maps

87. MAPS

1930. 1 map.

Political map of Allen County, showing roads, towns, and villages. John E. Breese, C.E., Lima, Ohio, publisher. Black and white. Scale,1 inch equals 1 mile. 42 x 31. County courthouse. Room 101.

The office of county surveyor, another English institution transplanted in America during the colonial period; became an important office in colonial Ohio where land titles and boundary lines were often in dispute. The office is purely a creature of statute, there being no constitutional provisions for its establishment.

The first act of the general assembly pertaining to the surveyor was passed during the first legislative session of 1803. Under this act the court of common pleas was authorized to appoint a person well qualified to act as county surveyor. He received his commission from the governor, was required to give bond conditioned for the faithful performance of the duties of his office; and was directed to survey all lands which were sold or were to be sold for taxes. The surveyor was authorized to appoint chain men or markers whose functions it was to establish corners. The surveys made by surveyor or his deputies were the only ones to be accepted as legal evidence in any court of law or equity. For remuneration, the surveyor was permitted to retain all fees collected by him in the operation of his office. (1 O.L. 90-93.)

The act of 1816, although making no fundamental change in the duties of the surveyor, fixed his term of office at five years; authorized him to appoint deputies and make him responsible for their official acts. Moreover he was made liable to removal by the court for negligence or incompetency, and was made liable to a suit by persons believing themselves damaged by his negligence or the negligence of his deputies. (14 O.L 112-225.) A year later, in1817, provision was made for the appointment of a successor in the event the office became vacant due to death, resignation or removal. (15 O.L. 65.)

The act of 1831 consolidated the previous acts, redefined the duties of the surveyor, increased the amount of his bond, and authorized him, when directed by the county commissioners, to procure from the surveyor general's office a certified plat together with the field notes. It provided further, that the surveyor should keep "a fair and accurate record of all official surveys made by him or by his deputies," in a suitable book to be kept by him for that purpose; and that he should number his surveys progressively. (29 O.L. 402.) More significant however was the fact that the office was made elective for a three-year term by the act of 1831. The term remained at three years until 1906 when it was to be reduced to a two year period. (29 O.L. 399; 98 O.L. 245-247.)

During the years of the development of the office other duties have been delegated to the surveyor. Thus in 1842 he was given the duty of ascertaining and reporting trespassing on public lands. (40 O.L. 57.) Two years later he was given the same powers as the justices of the peace to take and certify deeds, mortgages, powers of attorney, and other instruments affecting real estate, to administer oaths, and take affidavits and to certify them. (52 O.L. 70.) In 1867 he was given authority, when directed by the county commissioners, to transcribe any and all dilapidated maps, records of plats, and field notes of survey in other counties. (64 O.L. 216-217; 78 O.L. 258.) Similarly in 1881, he was authorized to procure from any office in the state a certified plat together with the field notes of corners, quarters sections, lot of original survey and place them in a book provided for that purpose. Certified copies from his book to be taken as *prima facie* evidence. (29 O.L. 399; 78 O.L. 85.)

With the increase in modern means of transportation there was a growing need for more effective methods of road construction and maintenance. Accordingly, in 1906, the surveyor was directed to act, whenever the services of an engineer were required, in the capacity of an engineer with respect to roads, turnpikes, bridges, or ditches, except in cities of the first grade. (98 O.L. 245-247.) Fourteen years later he was directed by statute to perform all duties in his county which would be done by a civil engineer or surveyor. He was directed further to prepare all plans, specifications and estimates of cost, and submit forms of contracts, for the construction and repair of all bridges, culverts, roads, draws, ditches, and other public improvement (except building) over which the county commissioners had authority. He was, at the same time, made responsible for the inspection of all public improvements, and was directed to keep a complete list of all estimates and bids received for such work as well as of contracts awarded for improvement. (98 O.L. 245-247.)

Similarly another measure, enacted in 1919, increased the duties of the surveyor regarding road construction and road maintenance. Under this act the surveyor was authorized to designate one of his deputies as maintenance engineer. This engineer, under the direction of the surveyor, was to have charge of all "road maintenance and repair work" in his county. It provided further that the surveyor, when authorized by the county commissioners, was to appoint a maintenance supervisor or supervisors to have charge of the maintenance of improved highways within a district or districts established by the commissioners or surveyor, and contain not less than ten miles of improved country roads. (108 O.L. Pt. 1, 497.) Four years later the surveyor was given the additional duty of assisting the county planning commission. (110 O.L. 312.)

Thus the general responsibility of planning and directing county road construction is vested, by statute, in the county surveyor. With this increased responsibility placed on this office there has been an attempt made to raise the general qualifications of those seeking election to it. Accordingly, in 1935, an act was passed changing the title of the office to that of "county engineer," and eligibility to the office was restricted to "professional and registered surveyors listed to practice in the state of Ohio." (116 O.L. 283.) This act was amended in 1936 to permit the incumbent to continue in office upon re-election, despite the lack of those qualifications.

Bills and Accounts

88. SURVEYOR'S MISCELLANEOUS RECORD
1924—. 3 vols.

Surveyor's record of miscellaneous bills and accounts. Alphabetical index in front of each volume. Indiscriminately handwritten and typed. Volumes average 600 pages. 16 x 12 x 2.5. County courthouse. Room 111.

89. FORCE ACCOUNT RECORD
1931—. 1 vol.

Record of orders from the county commissioners to the county surveyor for materials. Alphabetical index in front of volume. Handwritten. 25 pages. 16 x 10 x 1.5. County courthouse. Room 111.

90. UNPAID BILLS AND COPIES OF OFFICIAL LETTERS
1909—. 11 file boxes.

County engineer's copies of official letters and records of unpaid bills. Cardex system. 8 x 12 x 17. County courthouse. Room 111, in steel cabinet.

Bridges, Ditch and Road Records

91. DITCH ESTIMATE RECORDS
No date. 1 vol.

Stubs of surveyor's certificates of completed ditch contracts, listing name of surveyor, and date of completion. Alphabetical index in front of volume. Handwritten on printed forms. 200 pages. 16 x 12 x 1.5. County courthouse. Room 111.

92. BRIDGE CONTRACTS AND SPECIFICATION RECORD
1909—. 6 vols. (— 1911, missing.)

Record listing each contract number, name of contractor, estimated cost of material, and actual cost. Alphabetical index in front of each volume. Handwritten on printed forms. Volumes average 600 pages. 16 x 12 x 2.5. County courthouse. Room 111.

93. SURVEYOR'S ROAD CONTRACT RECORD
1911—. 21 vols. (— 1911, missing.)

Engineer's record of road building and repairing contracts. Alphabetical index in front of each volume. Indiscriminately handwritten and typed. Volumes average 600 pages. 16 x 12 x 2.5. County courthouse. Room 111.

94. SURVEYOR'S DITCH CONTRACT RECORD
1911—. 3 vols.

Record listing each contract number, name of contractor, estimated cost of labor and materials. Alphabetical index in front of each volume. Handwritten. Volumes average 600 pages. 16 x 12 x 2.5. County courthouse. Room 111.

95. FIELD NOTES, 1918-1920
1 vol.

Record of original government surveys in Allen County, Ohio. No index. Handwritten. 50 pages. 21 x 17 x .5. County courthouse. Room 111.

The office of clerk of courts, an ancient English institution originating before the time of Edward I (Sir Frederick Pollock and Frederic William Maitland, *The History of English Law Before the Time of Edward I*, 2 vols., Cambridge, 1895, I, 184.) was transplanted in America during the colonial period. The American Revolution made no radical change in the political heritage derived from England, and the office was continued by the states. The duties of the office were modified, however, due to the separation of administrative and judicial functions in the newer states, which under the English system had been combined.

The sections of the Ohio constitution of 1802 creating the judicial system for the state, provided for the appointment of a clerk of courts by the judges of the court of common pleas. He was to serve a seven-year term, but was subject to removal by the appointing power for a breach of good behavior. (*Ohio Const. 1802*; Art. III, sec. 9.) When, in 1851, a new constitution was adopted, the instrument made the office of clerk an elected one with a three-year term. (*Ohio Const. 1851*, Art. IV, sec 6.) A constitutional amendment in1905 provided that the term of all elective offices should be for an even number of years, not exceeding four. In compliance with the amendment, the general assembly passed an act fixing the term of the office of the clerk at two years. (98 O.L. 273.) The term remained at two years until 1935 when it was extended to four years. (116 O.L. pt. 2, 1st. sess. H. 603.) The remuneration of the office was by fees until 1906 when the legislature prescribed a definite salary. (98 O.L. 98, 117.)

The duties of the clerk of courts, like other county officers, were prescribed by statute. The code of civil procedure, adopted in 1853, summarized the earlier duties and laid the basis for the present day duties of the clerk. The duties as prescribed under this code were similar, in most respects, to those prescribed during the earlier years of the office. The clerk of courts was directed to issue all writs and orders for provisional remedies; endorse the date upon all papers filed in his office; keep the journal, record books and papers appertaining to the court and record its proceedings. Although the clerk had kept records during the earlier period he was directed to keep at least five books to be called the appearance docket, the trial docket and a printed duplicate of the trial docket, the journal, the record, and the execution docket. (51 O.L. 158-159; 78 O.L. 108; 79 O.L. 115; 86 O.L.174.) The present practice of keeping an index, direct and reverse, to judgments began in 1863. (63 O.L. 10; 75 O.L. 103; 78 O.L. 88; 82 O.L. 39; 86 O.L. 26.) Eight years later, in 1871, the clerk was made official custodian of the law reports and books furnished by the state for the use of the bar, and was made liable for their destruction. (68 O.L. 109.)

While the duties of the clerk as defined by the civil code of 1853 are still effective, other duties have been added by subsequent legislation. Thus, for example, in 1858 the clerk was directed to receive notary commissions for record. (55 O.L. 13; 93 O.L. 406; 115 O.L. 117.) He was required, also, to receive for record special police commissions (1867), trademarks (1883), partnership agreements (1894), index to judgments of federal courts (1898), bills of sales of motor vehicles (1921), and certificates of judgments to operate as a lien (1935). (64 O.L. 60: 80 O.L. 195; 91 O.L. 357; 92 O.L. 25; 93 O.L. 285.) On the other hand, many of the earlier duties of the clerk have been transferred to other departments of local government or have been abolished. The clerk issued marriage licenses, and ministers' licenses until 1851, after that date they were issued by the probate court. Moreover the clerk issued peddlers' licenses until the decade of the sixties, since that time they have been issued by the auditor. (59 O.L. 67.) The practice of recording the names of black or mulatto persons in the office of the clerk to be used as certificates of freedom was, of course, discontinued following the War Between the States.

The clerk of courts was given other duties in addition to those of serving the court of common pleas and receiving documents for record. Since 1850 he has been required to report annually to the county commissioners of all fines assessed by the court in criminal cases, together with the names of the parties to each case, and the amount of money he has paid to the treasurer. (48 O.L. 66; 58 O.L. 69; 86 O.L. 239.) Moreover, since 1867 he has been required to report annually to the secretary of state on the number of crimes committed in his county, the number of pending cases, together with the amount of fines collected. (64 O.L. 17.) An act of 1927, amending the act of 1867, directed the clerk to report on any matters which the secretary of state might require, and to forward a duplicate copy of his report on crime in his county to the state board of clemency. (Abolished, 1931.) (112 O.L. 203.)

The county clerk of courts, like the county prosecutor, is one of the important persons in the judicial system. His importance and influence was not recognized until recent years.

The court of common pleas, like many other county institutions, originated in England during the reign of Henry II (Adams, *op. cit.*, 109, 134.) Established in America during the colonial period, the office was continued by the states following the war of American Independence. The territorial act of 1788, establishing the American colonial policy in the Newer West in respect to the judiciary, contained sections authorizing the establishment of a common pleas court to be composed of not less than three nor more than five members. These members, appointed and commissioned by the territorial governor, were given jurisdiction in all civil matters. (Pease, *op. cit.*, 7.)

When a constitution was drafted for Ohio, in 1802, preparatory to the states entering the Union, provision was made for a continuation of the territorial court (*Ohio Const. 1802* Art. III, sec. 1.) The articles of the constitution, regarding the judiciary, provided for a court of common pleas to be composed of a president and associate judges. The members of the court, appointed by joint ballot of both houses of the general assembly, were to hold court in three judicial districts into which the state was to be divided by legislative action. (*Ohio Const. 1802*, Art. III, sec 3.) The court was assigned common law and chancery jurisdiction in all cases that should be provided by law. (*Ibid.*, Art. III, sec. 3.) To the court was assigned jurisdiction in probate and testamentary matters and in the appointment of guardians. Moreover, the court of common pleas and superior court were assigned original cognizance of criminal cases as might be provided by law (*Ibid.*, Art. III, sec. 4.) Appeals might be made from the county commissioners, justices of the peace, and other inferior courts in civil cases to the court a common pleas, (*Ibid.*, Art. III, sec. 3.) Finally, the court was authorized to appoint a clerk. (*Ibid.*, Art. III, sec. 6.)

Since the provision of the constitution called for legislative action, an act was passed in 1803 interpreting, the constitutional provisions. Under this act the court was given original jurisdiction in all cases in law and equity, when the matter and dispute exceeded the jurisdiction of the justices of the peace. The court was to take original cognizance of all probate, testamentary, and guardianship matters, and in all criminal matters exceeding the jurisdiction of the justices of the peace, except in cases where the punishment of the crime was capital. (1 O.L. 58.) A year later the jurisdiction of the court of chancery was restricted to cases where the sum involved was less than five hundred dollars. (2 O.L. 261.) In 1807 this restriction was removed, and the court was given original jurisdiction in all cases cognizable by a court of chancery, subject to an appeal to the supreme court. (5 O.L. 117.)

Meantime the court was assigned cognizance of criminal cases, wherein the punishment was capital, if the accused elected to be tried. (4 O.L. 57.) In 1810 the court was authorized to appoint a county prosecutor. (8 O.L. 165-167.) Ten years later the Chancery Act, adopted in 1810, conferred general chancery powers to the court (22 O.L. 75.)

Significant changes were made in the composition of the court and its jurisdiction during the middle of the nineteenth century. Under the constitution of 1851, the judges of the court of common pleas were made elected for a seven-year term. For the purpose of electing judges the state was divided into nine districts. The districts, of which Hamilton County constituted one, were to be composed of three or more counties. Each district, in turn, was to be subdivided into three parts, in each of which one common pleas judge was to be elected. Court was to be held in every district or county with such jurisdiction as should be fixed by law *(Ohio Const. 1851*, Art. IV, sec. 3,4.) Provision was made for the removal of judges by a concurrent resolution of two-thirds of the members elected to each house. (*Ibid.* Art. IV, sec. 17.)

The legislature, interpreting the constitutional provisions, made provision for judicial districts, but left the jurisdiction of the court much the same as it had been in the earlier years of its existence. (50 O.L. 70.) However, with the re-establishment of the probate court by constitutional provision, the court of common pleas was denied jurisdiction in cases of probate, testamentary, and guardianship matters. However the judgments and final decrees of the probate court could be reviewed by the court of common pleas on error. (51 O. L. 145.) A year later, in 1852, the court of common pleas was given original jurisdiction of all crimes and offenses, except minor criminal cases, the exclusive jurisdiction of which was invested in the justices of the peace or other minor courts. (R.S. 13422-5; 51 O.L. 474; 52 O.L. 73.)

During the same period the jurisdiction of the court, in certain communities, underwent a marked change. Thus in 1852, the criminal court of Hamilton County was re-established and to it was transferred the criminal jurisdiction formerly exercised by the court of common pleas. The latter court was given original cognizance of civil matters. (50 O.L. 90.) Shortly afterward the superior courts were re-established in Cincinnati, Franklin, and Montgomery counties. (52 O.L. 34; 53 O.L. 38; 54 O.L. 37.) Save in divorce, alimony, bastardy cases, the courts had the same jurisdiction as the court of common pleas.

At the opening of the twentieth century sweeping changes were again made in the organization of the courts. By the constitutional amendment of 1913, the divisions and subdivisions as provided by the constitution of 1851 were abolished. Provision was made for the election of one for more common pleas judges in each county. (*Const. of Ohio*, Art. IV, sec 3.) Ten years later provision was made for the selection of a chief justice of the court of common pleas. Under an act of March 13, 1923, in counties where there were two or more common pleas judges, they were authorized to designate one of their number as chief justice. The justice so designated by his colleagues was to serve in such a capacity until the expiration of his term, after which time the office of chief justice was to be an elective one. The elective section of the act was nullified by the supreme court on the grounds that the creation of a new elective official was unconstitutional. Accordingly, in 1927, an amendment was passed eliminating the elective feature of the act.

With the increased number of issues presented to the court of common pleas, the problems of judicial administration have become greater. This problem was solved in part by the creation of a chief justice of the court of common pleas who has been given the duties of superintending the business of the court, classifying it, and distributing it among the judges. Besides the duties enumerated the chief justice annually made a report to the clerk of courts showing the work performed by the court and by each judge in the proceeding calendar year. Moreover, he reports such other data as a chief justice of the supreme court may require. (G.C. 1558.)

Attempts have been made in recent years to improve the efficiency of the court by imposing stricter qualifications upon those who seek election to the bench. In 1917, and act was passed providing that a common pleas judge shall have been admitted to practice as an attorney and counsellor- at-law for a period of six years preceding his election. (107 O.L. 164.)

The court of common pleas has enjoyed a limited appointed power. Until 1833, the court was authorized to appoint a clerk of courts. Since 1915, the court has appointed a jury commission (which see). Other appointments, authorize doing the development of the office, are a court interpreter and a criminal bailiff. Since 1929, the court, and counties having a population in excess to 300,000, has been authorized to appoint one or more psychiatrists or psychologists or other examiners or investigators who shall hold their offices at the will of the court, and receive such compensation as a judge may determine, not exceeding the amount as may be appropriated by the county commissioners. (G.C. 1541; 113 O.L. 467.)

The records of the court of common pleas are deposited with the clerk of courts for safekeeping. He is made liable for the destruction of all law reports and books furnished by the state for the use of the court and the bar. (68 O.L. 109.)

Until 1851 the judicial power of the state of Ohio, in both matters of law and equity, was vested in the supreme court, court of common pleas, and justices' courts. The supreme court, during the first fifty years of Ohio history, served as a court of appeals, holding court in each county annually. When, in 1851, a new constitution was adopted, the judicial system was extended by the creation of district courts. These courts, composed of one supreme court justice and several common pleas judges in the district, were assigned original jurisdiction in the same matters as the supreme court, and such "appellate jurisdiction" as might be provided by law. (*Ohio Const. 1851*, Art. IV, sec. 5-6.) Thus by constitutional provision the courts were assigned original cognizance in *quo warranto, mandamus, habeas corpus*, and *procodendo* (*Ibid.*, Art. IV sec. 2.) In addition to this, the legislature, in 1852, authorized the courts to issue writs of error, *certiorari, super sedeas, no exeat*, and all other writs not specifically provided by statute, whenever such writs were necessary for the exercise of its jurisdiction. The same act gave the courts appellate jurisdiction from the court of common pleas, in civil cases, in which the court of common pleas had the original jurisdiction. (50 O.L. 68.)

For the purposes of the district courts, the nine common pleas districts were apportioned into five judicial districts. At the sessions of the district courts, a judge of the supreme court was designated to preside; in case no judge of the supreme court were present, as was often the case, the judge of the court of common pleas in whose subdivision court was being held was directed to preside. (50 O.L. 69.)

The district courts failed to function properly. Evidence seems to indicate that the ever increasing numbers of cases coming before the supreme court made it difficult for the justices to attend the meetings of the district courts. Indeed, six years before the creation of the district courts, the supreme court dockets were overcrowded. In 1845 the legislature found it necessary to afford relief, temporarily, by prohibiting appeals from the courts of common pleas to the supreme court. (43 O.L. 80.) A similar condition of overcrowding existed in the sixties. Thus, in 1865, the supreme court justices were relieved of duty of attending the meetings of the district courts for that particular year. (62 O.L. 72.) The judicial system had become slow and cumbersome. The courts declined rapidly after 1865 and were finally abolished in 1885. (62 O.L. 17-15.)

Following the complete collapse of the district courts an amendment to the constitution, adopted in 1883, made provisions for circuit courts. "The circuit courts," stated the amendment, "shall be the successor of the district courts, and all cases, judgments, records and proceedings pending in said district courts in several counties, shall be transferred to the circuit courts." (*Ohio Const.* Art. IV, sec. 6.) The courts were assigned the same "original jurisdiction with the supreme court, and such appellate jurisdiction as may be provided by law." The composition of the courts and the number of circuits was left to the discretion of the legislature. Accordingly, in 1884, an act was passed dividing the state into several circuits, and provision was made for the election of three judges in each circuit. (81 O.L. 170.)

The circuit courts, in addition to the jurisdiction conferred upon them by Art, IV, sec. 6 of the constitution, were authorized by the legislature to issue writs of *supersedeas* in any case, and all other writs not specially provided for, nor prohibited by statute, when they were necessary for the exercise of its jurisdiction. (81 O.L. 170.) Moreover the courts were authorized to make and publish rules of procedure in their respective circuits, as they deemed expedient, not in conflict with the law or rules of the supreme court. (81 O.L. 170.) On the other hand, the legislature directed that all cases taken to the circuit courts were to be entered on the docket in the order in which they were commenced, received or filed, and they shall, stated the law, "be taken up and disposed of in the same order." However, cases in which persons were seeking relief from imprisonment or persons who were convicted of a felony; cases involving the validity of any tax levy or assessment; cases involving the constitutionality of a statute; cases involving public right and proceedings in *quo warranto, mandamus, procedendo*, or *habeas corpus* (sic.), could be taken up in advance of their assignment or order on the docket. (81 O.L. 170.)

The judicial system of Ohio was again slightly changed in 1912. By an amendment to the constitution in that year the circuit courts were renamed courts of appeals. "The courts of appeals," stated the amendment, "shall continue the work of the respective circuit courts and all pending cases and processes in the circuit courts shall proceed to judgment and be determined by the respective courts of appeals." (*Ohio Const.* Art. IV, sec. 6.) The judges of the several circuit courts were designated as the judges of the courts of appeals, and were directed to perform the duties thereof until the expiration of their term of office. Vacancies, caused by the expiration of terms of office of the judges were to be filled by the electors of the respective appellate district. The term of office was fixed at six years.

The jurisdictions of the court remain much the same as it had been in 1851. However the court was assigned original cognizance in writs of prohibition (*Ohio Const.* Art. IV sec. 6.), and appellate jurisdiction in the trial of chancery cases. (*Ibid.*, Art. IV, sec. 6.) However, certain restrictions were imposed upon the court. No judgment of a court of common pleas or superior court or other court of record should be reversed except by "the concurrence of all the judges of the court of appeals." (*Ibid.*, Art. IV, sec. 6.)

At present the court consists of three judges in each of the nine districts into which the state is divided, each of whom shall have been admitted to practice as an attorney-at-law in the state for a period of six years immediately proceeding his election, one of whom is chosen every two years, and holds office for six years beginning on the ninth day of February next after his election. The salary of the circuit court judge, filed at $6,000 in per year in 1913, was increased to $8,000 in 1920 and so continues. (103 O.L. 418; 108 O.L. pt. 2, 1301.) The judges hold at least one session of court annually and each county in the district. (G.C. sec. 1, 514.)

Although the probation of prisoners had met with success at some eastern states and the latter part of the nineteenth century, it was not until 1908 that the first statute was passed in Ohio providing for the probation of convicted offenders. (For an interesting discussion of the development of probations see Louis N. Robinson, *Penology in the United States*, Philadelphia, 1922, 194-217.) The act authorized the courts to place convicted offenders, who, in the opinion of the judge, were not likely to again engage in crime or offensive conduct, on probation. This did not include, however, persons convicted of murder, arson, burglary, incest, sodomy, rape without consent, or the administration of poison. (99 O.L. 339.)

The plan met with immediate success. As a result of this success the legislature, in 1925, passed an act extending the system of probation. The act provides that the judge of the court of common pleas of a county or judges of such court and joint session, if they deem it advisable, may within the concurrence of the county commissioners establish a county department of probation. The department consists of a chief probation officer, and such other employees, clerks, and stenographers, as might be fixed by the judges. The judge or judges of the court of common pleas appoint all officers in the department, fix the salaries of the appointees, and supervise their work. The person appointed as probation officer must possess such training, experience and qualifications as may be prescribed by the department of public welfare. All positions within the department are in the classified service of the civil service of the county. (111 O.L. 424.)

The department has legal control and supervision of persons placed on probation and the county wherein the department is located and of any person resident within the county who may have been placed upon probation by any other court exercising criminal jurisdiction in a state whether within or without the county. Moreover, upon the request of the court, the probation department receives into legal custody any person paroled or conditionally paroled from a penal, reformatory, or correctional institution and remaining or residing in the county. The period of probation is determined by the court and may be extended, but not beyond a period of five years. (G.C. 13, 453-5; 113? O.L.)

The department is required to furnish to each person on probation or parole under its supervision or custody, a written statement of the conditions of probation and parole and instructs him and his obligations to society. Moreover the department is directed by law "to use all suitable methods, not inconsistent with the conditions of probation or parole, to aid and encourage such persons and bring about improvement in their conduct and condition." (111 O.L. 425.) The department is required, also, to keep informed concerning the conduct and conditions of each person and its custody. Persons on parole are required to report periodically to the county department and are visited regularly by members of the division.

Besides supervising and instructing probationers, the county department has the duty of keeping a detailed record of its work, an accurate and complete account of all moneys collected from persons under its supervision or in its custody; and to make such reports to the state department of public welfare as it may require.

In counties where there is no county probation department established, or where the trial court has no regular probation officer, the trial judge may designate some suitable person to act as a probation officer. This officer is required to make reports at designated periods, not less than once a month, concerning the conduct of the probationer in his charge. This officer is given the same power and is subject to the same rules as provided for regular constituted officers. (113 O.L. 123.)

In the event the probationer absconds during the period of his probation and is confined in any institution, the period of probation ceases to run until he is returned before the court. (G.C. sec. 13, 452-5; 113 O.L. 123.) During the period of probation, any field officer or probation officer may arrest the defendant without warrant and bring him before the judge before whom the case was pending. (111 O.L. 423; 113 O.L. 1231.) When the defendant is brought before the judge or magistrate, they may inquire into the conduct of the defendant, and may approve any sentence which might have been originally imposed or continue the probation. At the end of the probation period, the jurisdiction of the judge or magistrate ceases and the defendant is discharged and the judge may restore his citizenship.

Since the probation department is relatively new there is, to be sure, some inefficiency in administration. There is the argument, in some quarters, that probationers need no supervision. But authorities on criminal administration generally agree that suspension of sentences without supervision is not probation. Since the modification of the offenders behavior, rather than punishment, is the logic of probation, it is important that trained men be employed to supervise the activities of probationers; preferably not former policeman, who, because of their earlier training, are not always careful to make a distinction between the principles of supervision and discipline. Then, too, there is a need of scientific diagnosis by specialists in order to determine not only which individuals should be placed on probation, but also to determine the policies that should be used by the department in dealing with various classes of offenders. Finally, there is a growing need for well organized and centralized records. The entire record of previous crimes, as well as an educational and home record, should be carefully compiled, filed, and preserved for future reference.

Probation, in spite of its few defects, offers a solution for stamping out crime. Through such a system society learns what is needed to prevent men and women from becoming criminals, and the necessary steps to be taken to lead them back into normal society, after they have started a criminal career. (Robinson, *op. cit.*, 216.)

The office of coroner, next to the sheriff the oldest county office in America, had its inception in England during the latter part of the twelfth century. The coroner kept a record of the activities in the county, especially regarding criminal justice. At the end of the thirteenth century, it was his duty to make inquests whenever there was a sudden death in the shire, and the results were recorded in the coroner's rolls, and were presented to the justices when they made their eyre. (Sir Frederick Pollock and Frederic William Maitland, *The History of English Law Before the Time of Edward I*, 2 vols., Cambridge, 1895, I, 519, 571; II, 588, 641.)

This office, transplanted in America during the colonial period, was continued by the states following independence, and was adopted by the territory of which the state of Ohio was then a part. An ordinance of the Northwest territory, published in 1788, authorized the governor to appoint a coroner in each county within the territory. This act, together with a supplementary act of 1795 adopted from Massachusetts code, fixed the power and duties of the coroner. He was empowered to do any act which, by previous legislation had been delegated to the sheriff; he was given the ancient English duty of coroners in holding preliminary investigations over the bodies of all persons found within his county who were believed to have died by violence or casualties. (Theodore Calvin Pease, *The Laws of the Northwest Territory 1798-1800.* Ill. State Bar Assn., Law Ser., I, 24-25; 272-75.)

The Ohio constitution of 1802 continued historic office, making it elective for a two-year term. (*Ohio Const. 1802*, Art. VI, sec. I.) A statute of 1805 defined the duties and authority of the coroner which, in the main, were comparable to those prescribed in the territorial code. He was, however, denied the privilege of concurrent jurisdiction with the sheriff. (3 O.L. 156-161.) The act further provided that the coroner should receive his remuneration from fees; that if the office of sheriff were to become vacant due to death, resignation or otherwise, the coroner was to execute temporarily the duties of the sheriff. (3 O.L. 158-161.) The latter provision remained active until its abrogation in 1887 (84 O.L. 208-210.)

The constitution of 1851 and 1912 left the duties of the coroner unchanged and not until recent years, when he became an aid in the scientific detection of criminals, have any laws been passed which materially affected his office. By the legislative act of 1921 in all counties having a population of 100,000 or more only licensed physicians were eligible to the office and at the same time the coroner was made official custodian of the morgue. (109 O.L. 43-44.) In1927 an act was passed, apparently designed to attract more highly trained physicians, which set the salary of the coroner at $6,000.00 per year in all counties having a population of 400,000 or more inhabitants, and authorized him to appoint one stenographer, a secretary and three assistant custodians of the morgue. (112 O.L. 204-205.) Two years later the coroner was empowered to appoint a pathologist to serve as deputy coroner. The deputy was directed to make chemical test and to conduct autopsies. (113 O.L. 497.) In 1936 the tenure of the office was extended to two to four years. (G.C. sec. 2,823.)

Journals, Records, and Time Books

96. COURT ORDERS
1933. 1 vol.
This volume contains rules adopted by the common pleas court of Allen County. No index. Typed. 250 pages. 12 x 9 x 1.5. County courthouse. Room 208.

97. CIVIL CASES
1831—. 671 file boxes. 8 cartons. 8 shelves.
Papers of all civil cases and transcripts of cases. Indexed by separate volumes, see entry 98 and 99. File boxes, 5 x 10 x 10; cartons, 5 x 10 x 24; shelves, 5 x 10 x 6. County courthouse.
8 cartons, 8 shelves. Room 108.
623 file boxes. Room 208.
48 file boxes. Room 208A.

98. CIVIL RECORDS
1833—. 137 vols.
This is a common pleas court journal listing names of plaintiff and defendant, dates, findings, case numbers, and file box numbers. These volumes serve as an index to files of civil cases. Alphabetical index in front of each volume. 1838-1907, handwritten; 1908—, typed. Volumes average 600 pages. 16 x 12 x 3. County courthouse.
1933-1934. 132 volumes. Room 208.
1935—, 5 volumes. Room 208A

99. INDEX TO PENDING SUITS AND LIVING JUDGMENTS
1885—. 10 vols.
An index listing names of plaintiff and defendant, names of attorneys, case number, and file box number. Handwritten; Volumes average 600 pages. 18 x 13 x 3.5. County courthouse.
N.d. 1 volume. Room 400B.
1885-1895, 1 volume. Room 208.
1895—, 8 volumes. Room 208B.

100. BILLS OF THE EXCEPTION

No date. 4 file boxes, 1 carton.

These are bills of exception which have been filed. Indexed by separate volume, see entry 101. File boxes, 5 x 10 x 10; carton, 5 x 10 x 24. County courthouse.

1 carton (534-593). Room 108V.

4 file boxes (594-600). Room 208A.

101. BILL OF EXCEPTION

1902-1930. 1 vol.

A record of notice of filing bills of exceptions, listing dates, names of plaintiff and defendant, case number, and bill of exception number. No index. Handwritten on printed forms. 250 pages. 14 x 19 x 1. County courthouse. Room 208A.

102. JOURNAL ALLEN COUNTY COMMON PLEAS

1838—. 60 vols.

Descriptive record of cases kept by common pleas court. Volume A contains a supreme court record of applications for naturalization. Alphabetical index in front of each volume. 1838-1903, handwritten; 1903—, typed. Volumes average 600 pages. 18 x 15 x 3.5. County courthouse.

1831-1931 53, volumes. Room 208.

1932—. 7 volumes. Room 208A.

103. CHANCERY RECORD

1833-1856. 3 vols.

A common please court journal listing names of plaintiff, defendant, attorneys, dates, and case numbers. No index. Handwritten. Volumes average 500 pages. 18 x 11 x 3.5. County courthouse. Room 208.

104. CRIMINAL CASES

1831—. 12 file boxes, 11 cartons, 18 shelves.

A record of all criminal cases tried in common pleas court. Indexed by separate volume, see entry 107. File boxes, 5 x 10 x 10; cartons, 5 x 10 x 24; shelves, 6 feet long.

18 shelves, 11 cartons. Room 108V.

12 file boxes. Room 208.

105. CRIMINAL JOURNAL
1861—, 18 vols.

A criminal journal of Allen common pleas listing name of defendant, name of attorneys, dates, and action taken. Alphabetically index in front of each volume. 1861-1908, handwritten; 1908—, typed. Volumes average 600 pages. 18 x 13 x 3.5. County courthouse.

1861-1833, 17 volumes. Room 208.
1933—, 1 volume. Room 208A.

106. CRIMINAL RECORD
1833—. 17 vols.

A criminal record of Allen common pleas listing name of defendant, indictment, verdict, date, and case number. Alphabetical index in front of each volume. 1833-1908, handwritten; 1908—, typed. Volumes average 600 pages. 18 x 12 x 3. County courthouse.

1933-1925, 15 volumes. Room 208.
1926—, 2 volumes. Room 208A.

107. CRIMINAL JUDGMENT INDEX
1909- 1935. 1 vol.

A reverse index of criminal judgments, listing name of defendant, names of attorneys, dates, and nature of judgment and decision. Handwritten. 350 pages. 18 x 13 x 3. County courthouse. Room 208.

108. EXECUTIVE RETURN RECORDS
1865- 1881. 1 vol.

A record book of cases listing names of plaintiff and defendant, dates, and case numbers. Alphabetical index in front of volume. Handwritten. 450 pages. 18 x 12 x 3. County courthouse. Room 400B.

109. INDICTMENT RECORD
1888- 1914. 3 vols.

A record listing name of plaintiff, names of attorneys, nature of transaction, and the decision. Alphabetical index in front of each volume. Handwritten. Volumes average 100 pages. 18 x 12 x 1. County courthouse.

1889- 1893, 1895-1902, 1909-1920, 7 volumes. Room 400B.
1923- 1929, 1 volume. Room 208B.

110. JURY TIME BOOK

1889- 1929, 8 vols. (1894, 1903- 1908, 1921- 1922 missing.)

Record listing names of grand and petit jurors and dates of convening. No index. Handwritten. Volumes average 100 pages. 18 x 12 x 1. County courthouse.

1889- 1893, 1895- 1902, 1909- 1920, 7 volumes. Room 400B.

1923- 1929, 1 volume. Room 208B.

111. WITNESS BOOK

1859—. 21 vols. (1878-1879, 1909-1912, missing.)

Record listing names of plaintiff's and defendant's witnesses, jury, case number, dates, and cost. Alphabetical index in front of each volume.

112. TRANSCRIPTS

1903-1934. 11 file boxes.

Filed transcripts of Allen County common pleas court. Indexed by separate volumes, see entry 113. 5 x 10 x 10. County courthouse. Room 108V.

113. GENERAL INDEX

1833-1878. 2 vols.

Journal entries listing names of plaintiff and defendant, names of attorneys, terms of court, and case numbers. Indexed by key letters in front of each volume. Handwritten. Volumes average 600 pages. 18 x 12 x 2.5. County courthouse. Room 208.

Dockets

114. APPEARANCE AND EXECUTION DOCKET

1842—. 91 vols.

A record listing names of plaintiff and defendant, names of attorneys, action, title of case, findings, judgments orders, and decrees. Alphabetical index in front of each volume. 1842-1903, handwritten; 1903—, typed. Volumes average 600 pages. 18 x 13 x 3.5. County courthouse.

1842-1929, 1935—, 81 volumes. Room 208.

1929-1934, 10 volumes. Room 208B.

115. BAR DOCKET

1865-1879. 7 vols.

A record listing names of plaintiff and defendant, names of attorneys, pleadings, and case numbers. Alphabetical index in front of each volume. Handwritten. Volumes average 225 pages. 16 x 10 x 1.5. County courthouse. Room 400B.

116. CIVIL WITNESS DOCKET

1914-1934. 3 vols.

A record listing names of plaintiff and witnesses, defendant's witnesses, jury, dates, and case number. Jury time book is continued in 1929-1934 volume of this series. Alphabetical index in front of each volume. Handwritten and typed on printed forms. Volumes average 500 pages. 18 x 12 x 3.5. County courthouse.

1914-1929, 2 volumes. Room 208.

1929-1934, 1 volume. Room 208B.

117. CRIMINAL APPEARANCE AND EXECUTION DOCKET

1867—. 15 vols.

Allen County common pleas court record listing title of case, case number, names of attorneys, name of defendant, pleadings, findings, judgments, decrees, and amount of fees. Alphabetical index in front of each volume. Handwritten on printed forms. Volumes average 600pages. 18 x 15 x 3.5. County courthouse.

1867-1927, 11 volumes. Room 208.

1927—, 4 volumes. Room 208B.

118. CRIMINAL DOCKET

1863-1927, 52 vols. (1888, 1921-1922, missing.)

A criminal record listing statements of criminal cases, names of attorneys, name of defendant, dates, and judge's memorandum. Some alphabetically indexed in front of volume; others chronologically indexed. Handwritten. Volumes average 250 pages. 16 x 11 x 2. County courthouse. Room 400B.

119. CRIMINAL EXECUTION DOCKET

1860-1893. 6 vols.

A record listing name of defendant, charges, date, and remarks. Alphabetical index in front of each volume. Handwritten. Volumes average 450 pages. 18 x 13 x 3. County courthouse. Room 208.

120. CRIMINAL WITNESS DOCKET

1910—. 2 vols.

Common pleas court record listing names of plaintiff's and defendant's witnesses, names of jurors, dates, and case numbers. Alphabetical index in front of each volume. Handwritten. Volumes average 550 pages. 13 x 13 x 3. County courthouse.

1910-1919, 1 volume. Room 208.

1919—, 1 volume. Room 208B.

121. EXECUTION DOCKET

1934—. 1 vol.

A record listing case number and names of plaintiff and defendant. (One volume is blank.) Alphabetical index in front of each volume. Handwritten. Volumes average 300 pages. 16 x 14 x 2. County courthouse. Room 400B.

122. JUDGMENT DOCKET

1934—. 1 vol.

A record listing dates, amount, title of court, names of plaintiff and defendant, and decree. Alphabetical index in front of volume. Handwritten on printed forms. 500 pages. 18 x 12.5 x 3. County courthouse. Room 208B.

123. JUDGMENT INDEX, DIRECT

1865—. 9 vols.

Judgment index, direct, listing name of each judgment creditor, judgment debtor, date, and case number. Handwritten. Volumes average 600 pages. 18 x 13 x 3.5. County courthouse. Room 208.

124. JUDGMENT INDEX, REVERSE

1865—. 9 vols.

Judgment index, reverse, listing name of judgment debtor, judgment creditor, date, and name of each case. Handwritten. Volumes average 600 pages. 18 x 13 x 3.5. County courthouse. Room 208.

125. MOTION DOCKET

1861—. 20 vols. (1872-1873, 1895-1897, 1905-1909, missing.)

Record listing names of plaintiff and defendant, date of motion, and judge's memorandum. Chronologically arranged. Handwritten. Volumes average 200 pages. 16 x 11 x 1.5. County courthouse.

1861-1874, -1879-1904, 1910-1919, 16 vols. Room 400B.
1875-1878, 1 volume Room 400A.
1919—, 2 volumes. Room 208B.
No date. 1 volume. Room 208A.

126. PRAECIPE DOCKET
10 vols. (1888-1892, 1920-1924, missing.)

Record listing names of plaintiff and defendant, date, case number, order to clerk of court to issue execution papers to the sheriff. No index. Handwritten. Volumes average 300 pages. 14 x 10 x 2. County courthouse.
1868-1867, 1893-1919, 6 volumes. Room 400B.
1925-1934, 3 volumes. Room 208.
1934—, 1 volume. Room 208B.

127. TRANSCRIPT DOCKET
1903—. 3 vols.

Allen common pleas court record listing names of plaintiff and defendant, writs and sheriff's returns, names of attorneys, dates, judgments, and file box number. Alphabetical index in front of each volume. Handwritten on printed forms. Volumes average 600 pages. 18 x 13 x 3.5. County courthouse. Room 208B.

128. TRIAL DOCKET
1858-1917. 90 vols.

A record of Allen County common pleas court, listing names of plaintiff and defendant, and statement of case. Alphabetical index in front of each volume. Handwritten. Volumes average 250 pages. 16 x 11 x 2. County courthouse. Room 400B.

129. SECOND TRIAL DOCKET
1860-1870. 1 vol.

A common pleas second trial record listing names of plaintiff and defendant, names of attorneys, and time of case. Alphabetical index in front of volume. Handwritten. 250 pages. 14 x 11 x 2. County courthouse. Room 400B.

Probation Office

130. RECORD OF CASES

1931—. 4 file boxes.

A record of cases listing numbers, names, and decisions. Cardex system. 27 x 14 x 11. County courthouse. Room 307C.

Court of Appeals

General Court Records

131. JOURNAL

1913—. 2 vols.

A journal record of the court of appeals, Allen County, listing names of plaintiff and defendant, dates, and case numbers. Alphabetical index in front of each volume. Typed. Volumes average 600 pages. 18 x 12 x 3.5. County courthouse.

1913-1926, 1 volume. Room 208.

1926—, 1 volume. Room 208A.

132. LEGAL RECORDS

1911—. 29 file boxes.

Files containing various legal records of court of appeals. Indexed by separate volumes, see entry 134. 5 x 10 x 10. County courthouse.

1911-1928, 15 file boxes. Room 108.

1928—, 14 file boxes. Room 208A.

133. RECORDS COURT OF APPEALS

1911—. 40 file boxes.

Filed legal papers serving as a record of court of appeals. Indexed by separate volumes, see entry 134. 5 x 10 x 10. County courthouse.

1911-1928, 28 file boxes. Room 108V.

1929—, 12 file boxes. Room 208.

134. RECORD

1913—. 3 vols.

Court of appeals record, petitions and errors, listing names of plaintiff and defendant, and case numbers. Serves as an index to court of appeals files. Alphabetical index in front of each volume. Typed. Volumes average 600 pages. 18 x 12 x 3.5. County courthouse.

1913-1923. 1volume. Room 208.

1923—, 2 volumes. Room 208A.

135. RECORD OF CASES

1912—. 3 file boxes.

Record of cases pending and of cases tried before court of appeals. Cardex system. 20 x 7 x 4. County courthouse. Room 300A.

136. OPINIONS

1914-1935. 20 vols.

A record of opinions handed down by the court of appeals. No index. Typed on printed forms. Volumes average 200 pages. 14 x 9 x 1. County courthouse. Room 300A.

137. BRIEFS

1920—. 7 file boxes.

A record of briefs of cases before court of appeals for trial. Cardex system. 26 x 13 x 13. County courthouse. Room 300A.

138. APPEARANCE DOCKET

1913—. 2 vols.

Court of appeals record listing names of plaintiff and defendant, names of attorneys, action, pleadings, and cost. Alphabetical index in front of each volume. 1913-1827, handwritten on printed forms; 1927—, Typed on printed forms. Volumes average 350 pages. 18 x 13 x 2.5. County courthouse.

1913-1927, 1 volume. Room 208A.

1927—, 1 volume. Room 208B.

Supreme Court

Journals

139. SUPREME COURT RECORD
1837- 1864. 1 vol.
A journal of supreme court actions. No index. Handwritten. 450 pages. 16 x 10 x 2.5. County courthouse. Room 208.

Dockets

140. SUPREME COURT DOCKET
1845- 1867. 1 vol.
A record listing name of plaintiff and defendant, names of attorneys, and the findings. Chronological index. Handwritten. 200 pages. 12 x 8 x 1. County courthouse. Room 400B.

District Court

141. DISTRICT COURT JOURNAL
1861-1884. 2 vols. (— 1861, missing.)
A district court journal listing names of plaintiff and defendant, case number, and details of case. Alphabetical index in front of each volume. Handwritten. Volumes average 600 pages. 18 x 12 x 3.5. County courthouse.
1861-1882, 1 volume. Room 208.
1883-1884, 1 volume. Room 400B.

Circuit Court

General Court Records

142. JOURNAL
1885-1812, 3 vols.
Allen County circuit court journal of appeals and errors, listing names of plaintiff and defendant, and cases. Alphabetical index in front of volume. Handwritten and

typed. Volumes average 600 pages. 18 x 12 x 3. County courthouse.

1885-1899, 2 volumes. Room 400B.

1898-1902, 1 volume. Room 208.

143. LEGAL DOCUMENTS

1885-1912. 23 file boxes.

Filed legal documents of the circuit court. Indexed by separate volumes. 5 x 10 x 10. County courthouse. Room 108V.

144. RECORD

1885-1912. 7 vols.

Allen County circuit court records of petitions, listing names of plaintiff and defendant, dates, pleas, and errors. Alphabetical index in front of each volume. Handwritten. Volumes average 500 pages. 18 x 12 x 3. County courthouse.

1883-1896, 1902-1912, 3 volumes. Room 208.

1896-1901, 1903- 1912, 4 volumes. Room 400B.

Dockets

145. APPEARANCE DOCKET

1885-1911. 3 vols.

A record of Allen County circuit court listing names of plaintiff and defendant, names of attorneys, and pleadings. Alphabetical index in front of each volume. Handwritten. Volumes average 200 pages. 18 x 12 x 2.5. County courthouse.

1885-1909, 1 volume. Room 208.

1909-1911, 2 volumes. Room 400B.

146. TRIAL DOCKET

1885—. 6 vols. (1892-1907, missing.)

A record listing case numbers, names of plaintiff and defendant, date, judge's memorandum, records of circuit court and court of appeals. Indexed as to court term. 1885-1891, handwritten; 1908—, typed. Volumes average 400 pages. 16 x 12 x 2. County courthouse.

1885-1891, 1 volume. Room 400B.

1917-1925, 1908-1912, 2 volumes. Room 208.

1913-1916, 1926—, 3 volumes. Room 208A.

Cashier's Division

147. CASH BOOK

1855-1915. 12 vols. (1859-1865, 1872-1903, missing)

Cash accounts of Allen County common pleas court, listing names of payee and payor, cases, amounts. Some have alphabetical index in front and others have none. Handwritten. Volumes average 300 pages. 14 x 9 x 2. County courthouse. Room 400B.

148. CASH BOOK

1851—. 35 vols. (1860-1872, 1874, 1879, 1902, 1905-1908, missing.)

Cash accounts of clerk of courts listing names of payor and payee and amount paid. Alphabetical index in front of each volume. Handwritten. Volumes average 300 pages. 18 x 12 x 2. County courthouse.

1851-1859, 1873, 1875-1878, 1880-1901, 12 Volumes. Room 400B.

1903-1904, 1923-1925, 1909, 8 volumes. Room 400A.

1911-1925, 7 volumes. Room 108V.

1925—, 8 volumes. Room 208A.

149. DAY BOOK

1898-1899, 1913. 3 vols.

A record of cash accounts kept by Judge Klinger of the circuit court. No index. Handwritten. Volumes average 800 pages. 14 x 8 x 3. County courthouse. Room 400B.

150. CLERK'S FEE BOOK

1876-1895. 3 vols.

A record listing title of case and amount of fees. Alphabetical index in front of each volume. Handwritten. Volumes average 200 pages. 18 x 12 x 1.5. County courthouse. Room 400B.

151. RECORD OF ACCRUED FEES

1911-1932, 6 vols. (1921-1924, missing.)

The clerk's record of accrued fees, listing name of each fee, name of payee and amount. Alphabetical index in front of each volume. Handwritten on printed forms. Volumes average 300 pages. 18 x 12 x 1.5. County courthouse.

1911-1920, 4 volumes. Room 400B.

1925-1930, 1 volume. Room 208A.
1930-1932, 1 volume. Room 208B.

152. RECORD OF BONDS
1896—. 5 vols.

A record of bonds listing names and amounts, also purpose of bond. Alphabetical index in front of each volume. Handwritten and typed on printed forms. Volumes average 600 pages. 18 x 12 x 3.5. County courthouse.

1896-1913, 2 volumes. Room 400B.
1914—, 3 volumes. Room 208A.

153. UNCLAIMED COST
1878—. 5 vols. (1880-1881, 1885-1889, 1895-1905, missing.)

A record listing title of each action, docket, case number, amount, and date paid chronological index. Handwritten. Volumes average 200 pages. 16 x 11 x 2. County courthouse.

1878-1879, 1882, 1884, 1890-1894, 4 vols. Room 400B.
1906—, 1 volume. Room 208B.

154. CLERK'S VOUCHERS
1897—. 7 vols. (1899-1900, 1915-1918, missing.)

A record listing docket, number, clerk's name, and amounts of money. Alphabetical indexed in front of each volume. 1899-1908, handwritten; 1908—, typed. Volumes average 325 pages. 16 x 12 x 2.5. County courthouse.

1897-1898, 1901-1914, 4 volumes. Room 400B.
1919—, 3 volumes. Room 208A.

155. CANCELED CHECKS
n.d. 15 cartons.

Canceled checks of various public officials; also some alimony and support checks. 5 x 10 x 24. County courthouse. Room 108V.

156. CLERK'S CERTIFICATE
1873-1876. 2 vols.

These are books of stubs of clerk's certificates. No index. Handwritten. Volumes average 100 pages. 18 x 12 x 1. County courthouse. Room 400B.

Records of Motor Vehicles

157. BILLS OF SALE OF MOTOR VEHICLES
1921—. 468 file boxes.

Bills of sale of all motor vehicles sold in Allen County, listing names, dates, and description of motors. Indexed by separate volumes, see entry 158. 5 x 10 x 10. County courthouse. Room 208.

158. INDEX TO MOTOR VEHICLE SALES
1921—. 7 vols.

An index to bills of sale for all motor vehicles. Handwritten. Volumes average 600 pages. 18 x 15 x 4.5. County courthouse. Room 208.

Naturalization Records

159. RECORD OF DECLARATION OF INTENTION
1911-1929. 5 vols.

Certificates of declaration of intention to become citizens of the United States of America. Alphabetical index in front of each volume. Handwritten on printed forms. Volumes average 100 pages. 14 x 10 x 1. County courthouse. Room 208A.

160. PETITION AND RECORD, NATURALIZATION SERVICE
1907-1930. 4 vols.

A petition and record of information about the applicant. Alphabetical index in front of each volume. Handwritten on printed forms. Volumes average 150 pages. 20 x 12 x 1.5. County courthouse. Room 208A.

161. NATURALIZATION AND CITIZENSHIP PAPERS,
1928—. 15 file boxes.

A complete record containing certificates of declaration of intention, petitions and records, and certificates of naturalization. Alphabetically arranged. 2 x 18 x 24. County courthouse. Room 208A.

Records of Domestic Relations

162. ALIMONY AND DIVORCE RECORD
1913—. 1 file box.

Alimony and divorce records, listing plaintiff, defendant, alimony, and payment dates. Cardex system. 5 x 10.5 x 14. County courthouse. Room 208A.

163. ALIMONY RECORD
1917-1926. 2 vols.

A record of alimony, listing dates, names of plaintiff and defendant, and amount. (Ledger form of entry.) Alphabetical index in front of each volume. Handwritten. Volumes average 300 pages. 18 x 12 x 2. County courthouse. Room 208.

164. DIVORCE RECORD
1903-1913. 2 vols.

A record of divorces, listing names of plaintiff and defendant, address, decisions, and case numbers. Alphabetical index in front of each volume. 1903-1908, handwritten; 1908-1913, typed. Volumes average 600 pages. 18 x 12 x 3. County courthouse. Room 208.

Coroner's Record

165. INQUEST RECORDS
1902-1935. 22 file boxes.

A record of inquests held, listing names, dates, addresses, findings. Indexed by separate volume. 5 x 10 x 10. County courthouse. Room 108V.

166. CORONER'S RECORD
1923-1926. 2 vols.

A record of post-mortems, listing dates, names, addresses, and findings. Alphabetical index in front of volume. Handwritten on printed forms. Volumes average 300 pages. 14 x 9 x 1.5. County courthouse. Room 208.

167. CORONER'S INQUEST RECORD
1886—. 7 vols.

Record listing name of deceased, address, date and findings of each inquest. Alphabetical index in front of each volume. 1886-1890, handwritten; 1890—, handwritten on printed forms. Volumes average 325 pages. 16 x 11 x 2. County courthouse.

1886-1922, 4 volumes. Room 400B.

1923—, 3 volumes. Room 208.

Commissions and Licenses

168. RECORD A SPECIAL POLICEMAN'S COMMISSIONS

1925—. 1 vol.

A record listing authorization, oath, and certificate of special policeman. Alphabetical index in front of volume. Handwritten on printed forms. 300 pages. 14 x 9 x 1.5. County courthouse. Room 208B.

169. JUSTICE OF PEACE RECORD

1855—. 3 vols.

A record of justice's oaths, listing names, dates, and term of office. Alphabetical index in front of each volume. 1855-1871, handwritten, 1871—, handwritten on printed forms. Volumes average 300 pages. 14 x 9 x 1.5. County courthouse.

1855, 1 volume. Room 400A.

1861, 1 volume. Room 400B.

1909—, 1 volume. Room 208B.

170. NOTARIES' COMMISSION RECORD

1861—. 15 vols.

A record of notaries' commissions and oaths of office. Alphabetical index in front of each volume. Handwritten on printed forms. Volumes average 300 pages. 14 x 10 x 2. County courthouse.

1861-1934, 12 volumes. Room 202.

1934—, 3 volumes. Room 208B.

171. OPTOMETRY RECORD

1920. 1 vol.

Ohio State Board of Optometry records and certificates, listing names, dates, and place of practice. Alphabetical index in front of each volume. Handwritten on printed forms. 100 pages. 13 x 9 x .5. County courthouse. Room 208A.

172. RECORD OF HUNTERS' LICENSE

1913-1929. 7 vols. (1915-1920, 1924-1925, 1927-1928 missing.)

A record of hunting licenses listing name of each licensee, fee, and date of issue. Chronological indexed. Handwritten. Volumes average 300 pages. 14 x 9 x 1. County courthouse.

1926, 1929, 3 volumes. Room 208.

1913-1914, 1921-1923, 4 volumes. Room 400B.

173. FISHING LICENSE REGISTER

1916. 1 vol.

A record of fishing licenses, listing each license number, date, fee, and name of licensee. Chronological index. Handwritten. 250 pages. 16 x 12 x 1.5. County courthouse. Room 208.

174. REGISTER OF PARTNERSHIP

n.d.. 1 vol.

A record listing name of partnership, partner's names, and certificate number. Alphabetically arranged as to names. Handwritten. 250 pages. 16 x 12 x 2. County courthouse. Room 208A.

175. REGISTER OF REAL ESTATE LICENSES

1935—. 1 vols.

A record listing name of each licensee, license number, employing broker, and date of issue. Alphabetical index in front of volume. Handwritten. 500 pages. 18 x 13 x 3. County courthouse. Room 208A.

Miscellaneous Records

176. ESTRAY DOCKET

1895-1911. 1 vol.

A notice of receipt of stray animals. Alphabetical index in front of each volume. Handwritten. 250 pages. 16 x 11 x 2. County courthouse. Room 400B.

177. CLERK'S RECEIPT FOR PAPERS

1880. 1 vol.

A record listing names of attorneys and papers taken from the files. No index. Handwritten. 400 pages. 14 x 10 x 2. County courthouse. Room 400B.

178. MISCELLANEOUS PAPERS

No date. 7 cartons.

These boxes contain hunting license stubs, receipts, and books of jury witness fee stubs, grand jury witness vouchers, and other miscellaneous papers. No index. 5 x 10 x 24. County courthouse. Room 108V.

179. JUSTICE CRIMINAL DOCKET

1875-1910. 9 vols. (—, 1875, 1881-1885, missing.)

A record of warrants, subpoenas, showing trial dates and case numbers. Alphabetical index in front of each volume. Handwritten on printed forms. Volumes average 300 pages. 18 x 12 x 3. County courthouse. Room 400B.

180. JUSTICE CIVIL DOCKET

1856-1922. 152 vols.

A record listing judgment amount claimed, name of defendant and plaintiff, cost, and case number. Alphabetical index in front of each volume. Handwritten and typed. Volumes average 350 pages. 16 x 12 x 2. County courthouse. Room 400B.

The judicial system for the territory comprising the present state of Ohio established a probate court. This court, established by an act of the Northwest territory on August 30, 1788, consisted of a probate judge with jurisdiction in probate and testamentary and guardianship matters, and two judges of the court of common pleas, who sat with him and ruled on contested points, defective sentences, and final judgment. (Pease, *op., cit.*, 9.)

The judicial system established in 1803, under the first constitution of Ohio, made no provision for a probate court but invested such powers as had been exercised by the court in the territorial period in the court of common pleas. The constitution of 1851 recreated the probate court and gave it original jurisdiction of all probate and testamentary matters, and the appointment and supervision of guardians, and such other jurisdiction as might be provided by law. (*Ohio Const. 1851*, Art. IV. Sec. 8.) An amendment in 1912 authorized the common pleas judge, when petitioned by ten percent of the qualified voters in counties having a population less than 60,000, to submit the question of combining the probate court and the court of common pleas to the voters at any general election. (*Ohio Const.* Art. IV. Sec. 7.)

One of the primary functions of the court since its inception has been the settlement of the estates. By the civil code, adopted in 1853, the court was given original jurisdiction in taking proof of wills, in granting letters testimony, and in settling accounts of executors and administrators. (51 O.L. 167.) Until 1854 the court had jurisdiction in the matter of enforcing the payment of debts and legacies of deceased persons. While the court retains the original jurisdiction regarding estates, new duties have been added in recent years. With the development of inheritance tax laws as a new means of taxation the probate court has been required to determine and assess the tax after the county auditor has appraised the decedent's estate. (108 O.L. pt. 1, 561.)

By the constitutional provision the probate court has original jurisdiction in granting marriage licenses to ministers to solemnize marriages. The former provision was modified by an act, adopted in 1931, which requires an elapse of at least five days between the time of application and the issuance of marriage licenses. (114 O.L. 93.) Closely related to this function is the court's jurisdiction in cases of domestic relationships. In 1894 the probate courts in Allen, Richland, Perry, Defiance, and Wood counties were given jurisdiction in "divorce, alimony, foreclosure, and partition cases." (91O.L. 799.) This jurisdiction, later extended to other counties, was abolished in Hamilton, Lucas, Mahoning, Montgomery, Stark, Summit, and Franklin counties between the years 1911-1927 when an additional judge of the court a common pleas was elected and given jurisdiction in cases involving domestic relations. (See court of domestic relations.)

The jurisdiction of the court extends to the state's unfortunates. The constitution of 1851 gave the court jurisdiction in making inquests respecting lunatics, insane persons, and idiots. The constitutional provision in this respect was interpreted by the civil code of 1853. Since 1855 the court has been given jurisdiction in the appointment of guardians for minors, idiots, imbeciles, lunatics, and other incompetents by reason of advanced age. A year later, the court was authorized to commit persons who were mentally incompetent to state institutions maintained for such purposes. (53 O.L. 891.) In recent years the court has been given jurisdiction in trial cases involving neglected, dependent, and delinquent children. (See Juvenile Court.) In certain counties, however, this jurisdiction has been transferred to the newly established courts of domestic relations.

During the early years of its existence the court was given limited criminal jurisdiction in cases in which the sentence did not impose capital punishment or punishment by imprisonment. By the code of civil procedure (1853) the judgments and final decrees of the probate court could be reviewed by the court of common pleas on error. (51 O.L. 146.) In 1857 the criminal jurisdiction of the probate court was transferred to the court of common pleas (54 O.L. 97.) but later acts retained it in certain counties only. The last vestige of criminal jurisdiction disappeared with the adoption of the probate code in 1931. (114 O.L. 475.)

Miscellaneous duties, remotely related to the probate and testamentary matters, have been added by legislative action. Since 1888 the court has been required to file a certified list of all unknown depositors as furnished by institutions or persons engaged in loaning money for profit. (85 O.L. 65.) The present duty of changing the names of persons who desire it had its beginning in 1898. (92 O.L. 21.) Since 1908 the probate court has been required to file certificates of doctors and surgeons, and since 1916 the certificates of registered nurses which authorizes them to practice their profession in the county. (99 O.L. 499; 106 O.L. 193.) Since 1913 the court has been invested with the power to grant injunctions (103 O.L. 427.), and since 1915 has had concurrent jurisdiction with a court of common pleas in condemnation proceedings for roads. (105 O.L. 583.)

The probate judge, aside from his authority to appoint guardians and administrators, has enjoyed an additional appointing power which was conferred upon him by a legislative act of 1861. Under the provisions of this act he was, and, is authorized to appoint one gager and inspector of spirits, linseed, lard and coal oil; one inspector of flour and meal; one inspector of beef, pork, lard, and butter; one inspector of sawyer lumber and shingles; and one inspector of salt. (58 O.L. 105.) Since 1913 he has had authority to appoint members of the county board of visitors (which see), and since 1917 the city boards of park commissioners. (103 O.L. 173-174, 888; 107 O.L. 65.)

The probate judge, like other county officials, has been required by statute to keep a record of the business of his office. The present system of records, originating for the most part in 1853 and continued by the probate code of 1931, includes a criminal record, an administrative docket, a guardian's docket, a marriage record, a record of bonds, a naturalization record, and a permanent record of births and deaths. (51 O.L. 167; 52 O.L.103; 75 O.L.9; 114 O.L. 324.)

The probate judge has the care and custody of files, papers, books and records belonging to the probate office. The probate code, adopted in 1931, directed the probate judge to preserve for further reference and examination all pleadings, accounts, vouchers, and other papers in each estates, trust, assessment, and guardianship, or other proceedings. Such papers are to be properly jacketed and tied together. Moreover, he is required to make proper entries and indexes omitted by his predecessors. Certificates of marriages, reports of births and similar papers not a part of a case or proceeding are to be arranged and preserved separately in the order of dates and which they are filed. (114 O.L. 321-322.)

At present the probate judge is elected for a four-year term. (114 O.L.320.) In recent years there has been an attempt to raise the qualifications of those seeking elections to this office. Accordingly, in 1935 the probate code of 1931 was amended and eligibility to the office was restricted to practicing or to a person who *"shall have previously served as a probate judge immediately prior to his election."* (116 O.L. 481.)

The juvenile court, though of uncertain origin, has been generally recognized as an American contribution to the administration of social justice. The establishment of such courts was the logical outcome of the practical philosophy of enlightened public men that child offenders against the law, or conventional social standards, should not be treated as criminals, but as unfortunates needing the help, supervision, and protection of the state. (Miriam Van Waters, *Youth in Conflict*, New York, 1925, 147, 159, 161.) Although the idea of a separate court for the trial of juvenile offenders was an institution of gradual growth, the first court of this kind in the United States was established in 1899, in Cook County, Chicago, Illinois, by an act of the legislature of that state. The Illinois experiment gave an impetus to the children's movement in the middle west. (Edward H. Sutherland, *Principles of Criminology*, Chicago, 1934, 270-272.)

The Ohio Legislature was not slow in seeing the advantages of the Illinois experiment, and accordingly, in 1902, an act was passed creating the juvenile court in Cuyahoga County. Under this act all counties having a population of over 380,000 and an insolvency court was authorized, under an extension of the jurisdiction of this court, to establish children's courts. It gave the court jurisdiction of the trial of cases involving delinquent and neglected children; define the terms "delinquent, dependent, and neglected"; authorized the appointment of a probation officer, and made it his duty to investigate the facts of cases coming before the court, and to take charge of the offender before and after trial. The clerk of the juvenile court was directed to keep a journal in which was to be recorded the minutes of the case. The judge was to serve for a period of five years. (95 O.L. 785.) The term remained at five years until 1935 when it was extended to six years.

Two years after the establishment of the Cuyahoga County juvenile court, the assembly provided, by statute, for the establishment of juvenile courts in the rural counties of the state which, because of their lack of population, were unable to create the newer agencies under the provision of the act of 1902. Under the act of 1904 the judges of the court of common pleas, probate court, and where established, the insolvency courts, wherein three or more judges held court concurrently, were authorized to appoint one of there members as "juvenile judge." The court was given original jurisdiction in all cases involving neglected, dependent and delinquent children under the age of sixteen years; and all children, who, in the past, had been scheduled for trial in a justice of the peace or police court were in the future to be tried before a juvenile judge. As under the act of 1902, the judge was authorized to appoint a probation officer, and the clerk of courts was directed to keep a journal of the minutes of each case. (97 O.L. 561.) In 1908 the court was given jurisdiction in cases involving minors under seventeen years of age, and, such children as were brought before the juvenile judge were to become wards of the court until they had attained the age of twenty-one years. Moreover, the county commissioners were authorized to provide by lease or purchase a "detention home" where neglected or dependent children might be detained pending the final disposition of their cases. The clerk of courts was directed to keep not only a journal, but also an appearance docket containing all orders, judgments, and findings of the court. It provided, also, for case studies to be made by the probation officer. (99 O.L. 196.) The age jurisdiction of the court was increased to eighteen in 1913. (103 O.L. 877.)

While provisions were being made for the establishment of juvenile courts, the legislature gave the court jurisdiction in cases involving adults who committed crimes against children or contributed to the delinquency of dependent children. Thus in 1906 it was made a misdemeanor to contribute to the delinquency of a child under eighteen years of age. (98 O.L. 314.) Two years later the "lack of parental care" was defined and it was made a misdemeanor to fail to support a minor, or to cause him to engage in begging. (99 O.L. 196.) In 1913 "proper parental care" was defined by statute. (103 O.L. 877.)

Marked progress has been made in the medical treatment of juveniles. While the act of 1913 authorized the juvenile judge to submit any child sentenced to an institution for correction to a mental test, the act of 1929 authorized him to submit any child coming before the court to a mental and physical test to be made by a physician or psychiatrist. (103 O.L. 872; 113 O.L.471.) To further the scientific handling of children, the county commissioners were authorized, in the same year, to lease or construct a separate building to be known as the "juvenile court" which should be appropriately constructed, arranged, furnished and maintained for the convenience and effective transition of the business of the court, including adequate facilities to be used as laboratories, dispensaries or clinics for the scientific use of specialists attached to the court. (113 O.L. 470.)

One of the guiding principles of the court has been to make its "custody and discipline" of children approximate as nearly as possible that which should be given by their parents. In the cases involving neglected or dependent children, not sentenced to state institutions, it has been the policy of judges to assign children to private homes, and make arrangements for their adoption.

Many other functions have been taken over by the juvenile court such as mothers' pensions. (103 O.L. 877.)

The juvenile court of Cuyahoga County is the only independent juvenile court in the state. There are seven other juvenile courts in Ohio, all attached to the court of domestic relations. In smaller counties the probate judge is assigned all juvenile cases.

Journals and Case Records

181. JOURNAL, PROBATE COURT
1837-1931. 44 vols.
A record of court proceedings listing case numbers, dates, and name of parties involved. Alphabetical index in front of each volume. 1837-1902, handwritten; 1902-1931, typed. Volumes average 500 pages. 16 x 10 x 2.5. County courthouse. Room 206.

182. PROBATE JOURNAL
1852-1934. 14 vols. (1859-1894, missing.)
A journal listing appointments and filings of probate court. Alphabetical index in front of each volume. 1852-1907, handwritten; 1908-1934, typed. Volumes average 600 pages. 18 x 12 x 2. County courthouse. Room 206.

183. CIVIL RECORD, PROBATE COURT
1852-1935. 55 vols.
A record of civil proceedings of the probate court, listing case number, names of parties, names of attorneys, and findings. Alphabetical index in front of each volume. 1852-1908, handwritten; 1908-1935 typed. Volumes average 500 pages. 16 x 10 x 2.5. County courthouse. Room 206.

184. CRIMINAL JOURNAL
1866-1921. 2 vols.
A record of criminal proceedings, listing cases, names and findings. Alphabetical index in front of each volume. Handwritten. Volumes average 350 pages. 16 x 12 x 2. County courthouse. Room 206.

185. GENERAL INDEX
No date. 1 vol.
A general index to estates and civil cases of probate court. Handwritten. 400 pages. 20 x 14 x 2. County courthouse. Room 206.

186. COMMISSIONERS' RECORD OF INSOLVENCY
1891-1928. 1 vol.

A record of proceedings had before commissioners of insolvents, listing names, addresses, dates, and amounts. No index. Handwritten. 320 pages. 16 x 12 x 2. County courthouse. Room 206.

187. RECEIPT FOR PAPERS
1891. 1 vol.

A record of receipts for each paper taken from the files listing date, name of person, title of the paper. Alphabetical index in front of volume. Handwritten. 150 pages. 16 x 12 x 1.5. County courthouse. Room 400B.

188. AFFIDAVITS TO PATENT RIGHTS
1868-1869. 1 vol.

Probate court record of affidavits to patent rights, listing dates and names. No index. Handwritten on printed forms. 400 pages. 14 x 12 x 3. County courthouse. Room 400A.

189. INVENTORIES AND SALES BILLS
1837—. 47 vols.

Record of inventories and sales, listing dates, names, and amounts. Alphabetical index in front of each volume. Handwritten. Volumes average 600 pages. 14 x 12 x 2.5. County courthouse. Room 206.

190. JOURNAL AND RECORD OF CORONER'S INVENTORY
1899-1926. 1 vol.

A record of coroner's inquest, listing names, addresses, and findings. Alphabetical index in front of volume. Handwritten. 200 pages. 14 x 12 x 2. County courthouse. Room 206.

191. MISCELLANEOUS BONDS
1900-1920. 1 vol. (— 1900, missing.)

A record of various bonds listing names, dates and amounts. Alphabetical index in front of volume. Handwritten. 300 pages. 16 x 12 x 2. County courthouse. Room 206.

192. WITNESS BOOK
1866-1919. 3 vols.

A record listing names of jurors and witnesses of probate court. Alphabetical index in front of each volume. Handwritten. Volumes average 350 pages. 16 x 12 x 2.5. County courthouse. Room 206.

Calendars and Dockets

193. PROBATE COURT CALENDAR
1900-1905. 6 vols.

Probate court calendar listing number and date of each case. Alphabetical index in front of each volume. Handwritten. Volumes average 75 pages. 18 x 12 x 1. County courthouse. Room 400B.

194. MATURITY CALENDAR
1913-1916. 1 vol.

A record listing case number, accountant, amount due, and when notified. No index. Handwritten. 200 pages. 16 x 12 x 2. County courthouse. Room 206.

195. SETTLEMENT CALENDAR
1899-1910. 4 vols. (1894-1900, missing.)

A record of settlements made by administrators, listing names, amounts, and dates. Chronologically arranged. Handwritten. Volumes average 200 pages. 16 x 14 x 1.5. County courthouse.

1899-1894, 2 volumes. Room 400B.
1901-1910, 2 volumes. Room 206.

196. ADMINISTRATOR'S DOCKET
1849-1929, 15 vols.

A record of appointments of guardians and administrators listing names, dates, and addresses. Alphabetical index in front of each volume. 1849-1908, handwritten; 1908-1929 typed. Volumes average 400 pages. 16 x 12 x 2.5. County courthouse. Room 206.

197. APPEARANCE DOCKET

1872-1934. 19 vols. (— 1872, missing.)

A record listing names of parties, dates of filing, and remarks. Alphabetical index in front of each volume. 1872-1908, handwritten; 1908-1934 typed. Volumes average 500 pages. 16 x 12 x 2.5. County courthouse. Room 206.

198. ASSESSMENT DOCKET

1878-1901. 3 vols.

A record of assessments listing case number, names of parties, dates, and amounts. Alphabetical index in front of each volume. Handwritten on printed forms. Volumes average 300 pages. 16 x 12 x 2.5. County courthouse.

1878-1886, 1 volume. Room 400B.

1884-1901, 1886-1895, 2 volumes. Room 206.

199. CRIMINAL TRIAL DOCKET

1863-1932. 5 vols. (2 series of vols. covering approximately the same dates.)

A record of criminal trials and proceedings, listing case numbers, names, and findings. Alphabetical index in front of each volume. Handwritten. Volumes average 500 pp 16 x 12 x 2.5. County courthouse. Room 206.

200. DOCKET

1836-1849. 2 vols.

A petitions to sell land, listing names, dates and description of land. Alphabetical index in front of each volume. Handwritten. Volumes average 300 pages. 13 x 9 x 2. County courthouse. Room 206.

201. EXECUTION DOCKET

1853-1892. 1 vol.

A record of judgments and cost listing case numbers, names, and amounts. Alphabetical index in front of volume. Handwritten. 400 pages. 14 x 12 x 2.5. County courthouse. Room 206.

202. MOTION DOCKET
1883-1921. 4 vols.
A record of probate court motions. Alphabetical index in front of each volume. Handwritten. Volumes average 200 pages. 16 x 14 x 2. County courthouse.
1883-1895, 1901-1921, 3 volumes. Room 206.
1895-1901, 1 volume. Room 400B.

Fiscal Accounts

203. CASH BOOK
1883-1932. 16 vols.
A cash record of receipts and disbursements, listing dates, names, and amounts. Alphabetical index in back of volume. Handwritten. Volumes average 300 pages. 16 x 12 x 2. County courthouse. Room 206.

204. CASH JOURNAL
1916-1918. 1 vol. (— 1916, missing.)
A cash account listing amounts received, and from whom. Indexed by separate volume, see entry 205. Handwritten. 600 pages. 12 x 10 x 3. County courthouse. Room 206.

205. JOURNAL INDEX
n.d. 1 vol.
A general index to the cash journal. Handwritten. 500 pages. 18 x 14 x 3. County courthouse. Room 206.

206. EXAMINATION REPORTS, COUNTY TREASURER
1894. 1 vol.
Examination record of treasury conditions listing receipts and expenditures. Alphabetical index in front of volume. Handwritten on printed forms. 200 pages. 18 x 12 x 1.5. County courthouse. Room 206.

207. RECORD OF ACCOUNTS
1844-1935. 63 vols.
A record of official proceedings and accounts of probate court listing names, cases, and amounts. Alphabetical index in front of each volume. 1844-1908, handwritten;

1908-1935, typed. Volumes average 600 pages. 16 x 12 x 2.5. County courthouse. Room 206.

208. RECORD OF FEES

1871-1882. 2 vols.

A record of money received for court fees listing names of parties and amounts. Alphabetical index in front of each volume. Handwritten. Volumes average 450 pages. 18 x 12 x 3. County courthouse.

1871- 1882, 1 volume. Room 206.

1882, 1 volume. Room 400B.

209. RECORD OF ACCRUED FEES

1907-1931. 4 vols.

Probate court record of accrued fees listing names, dates, and amounts. No index. Handwritten. Volumes average 250 pages. 16 x 13 x 1. County courthouse. Room 206.

210. CERTIFICATES OF FEES

1919-1924. 1 vol.

Stubs of certificates of fees issued by probate court. No index. Handwritten on printed forms. 300 pages. 15 x 14 x 2. County courthouse. Room 206.

211. COST BILL RECORD EXTENDED JURISDICTION

1896-1900. 1 vol.

Cost bill petitions, foreclosures, divorce and alimony records, listing names, cases, and amounts. No index. Handwritten. 350 pages. 14 x 12 x 2. County courthouse. Room 400B.

212. JUVENILE COST BILL RECORD

1907-1910. 1 vol.

A record of juvenile court cost bills, listing names, case numbers, and amounts. Alphabetical index in front of volume. Handwritten. 200 pages. 18 x 11 x 1.5. County courthouse. Room 400B.

213. RECORD OF UNCLAIMED DEPOSITS

1926. 1 vol.

A record of deposits not claimed by owners listing dates and amounts. Alphabetical index in front of volume. Handwritten on printed forms. 350 pages. 18 x 14 x 2.5. County courthouse. Room 206.

214. JOURNAL OF SETTLEMENTS
1879-1934. 11 vols

A record of the court settlement of accounts, listing names, dates, and amounts. Alphabetical index in front of each volume. 1879-1908, handwritten on printed forms; 1908-1934, typed on printed forms. Volumes average 600 pages. 18 x 13 x .25. County courthouse. Room 206.

Bonds, Letters, and Records of Fiduciaries and Estates

215. APPOINTMENT OF ACCOUNT RECORD
1837-1906. 8 vols.

A record of appointment of estate administrators, executors, and guardians listing names, dates, estates, and amount of each bond. Alphabetical index as to estates in front of each volume. Handwritten on printed forms. Volumes average 600 pages. 16 x 12 x 2.5. County courthouse. Room 206.

216. RECORD OF ASSESSMENTS, BONDS, AND APPRAISEMENTS
1882-1896. 2 vols.

A record of appointments listing names, assignments, bonds, and appraisements. Alphabetical index in front of each volume. Handwritten. Volumes average 450 pages. 15 x 13 x 2.5. County courthouse. Room 206.

217. ASSIGNEES' BONDS AND LETTERS
1876-1934. 3 vols.

A record of assignment of property listing dates, names, and giving descriptions of property. Alphabetical index in front of each volume. Handwritten on printed forms. Volumes average 250 pages. 16 x 14 x 2. County courthouse. Room 206.

218. RECORD OF BONDS AND APPOINTMENTS - ESTATES
1882-1934. 21 vols.

A record of bonds, estates, and appointments listing names, addresses, and amounts. Alphabetical index as to estates in front of each volume. Handwritten and typed. Volumes average 600 pages. 18 x 12 x 3. County courthouse. Room 206.

219. GUARDIAN BONDS
1859-1883. 4 vols.

A record of bonds executed listing names, dates, and amounts. (There may be some volumes missing as dates are uncertain.) Alphabetical index in front of each volume. Handwritten on printed forms. Volume average 500 pages. 16 x 12 x 2.5. County courthouse. Room 206.

220. BOARD OF GUARDIAN INVENTORY
1883-1935. 2 vols.

A record of guardians' inventories listing names and amounts. Alphabetical index in front of each volume. Handwritten. Volumes average 500 pages. 16 x 13 x 2.5. County courthouse. Room 206.

221. FINAL RECORD OF ACCOUNTS
1837-1846. 1 vol.

A record of final settlement of accounts of estates listing names, amounts, dates, etc. Alphabetical index in front of volume. Handwritten. 300 pages. 14 x 11 x 2. County courthouse. Room 206.

222. GUARDIAN FUNDS AND LETTERS
1886—. 9 vols.

A record of bonds and letters of guardians pertaining to their guardianships. Alphabetical index in front of each volume. Handwritten. Volumes average 500 pages. 16 x 13 x 2.5. County courthouse. Room 206.

223. COST BILL RECORD ESTATES
1888-1910. 10 vols.

A cost bill record of appointment of administrator and executor listing names of parties, names of estates, amounts of costs, and dates. Alphabetical index in front of each volume. Handwritten on printed forms. Volumes average 600 pages. 18 x 12 x 2.5. County courthouse. Room 400B.

224. SCHEDULE OF DEBTS
1932—. 2 vols.

A record of debts against estates listing names of estates and amount of debts. Alphabetical index in front of each volume. Typed. Volumes average 600 pages. 15 x 13 x 3. County courthouse. Room 206.

225. RECORD OF WILLS
1836—. 21 vols.

A record of wills probated in Allen County. Alphabetical index in front of each volume. 1836-1907, handwritten; 1908—, typed. Volumes average 500 pages. 16 x 10 x 1.5. County courthouse. Room 206.

226. INHERITANCE TAX RECORD AND JOURNAL
1923-1934. 14 vols.

A record of inheritance tax listing names, dates, and amounts. Alphabetical index in front of each volume. Typed. Volumes average 600 pages. 18 x 12 x 3. County courthouse. Room 206.

Naturalization Records

227. NATURALIZATION RECORD
1857-1906. 13 vols.

A record of declarations of intention, first papers, and complete record of naturalization of aliens. Alphabetical index in front of each volume; Also indexed by separate volume, see entry 228. Handwritten and handwritten on printed forms. Volumes average 476 pages. 14 x 10.5 x 2.25. County courthouse. Room 206.

228. INDEX TO NATURALIZATION RECORDS
1844-1894. 1 vol.

An index to records of naturalization. Handwritten. 200 pages. 15 x 14 x 1.5. County courthouse. Room 206.

Vital Statistics

229. RECORD OF BIRTHS
1869-1909. 4 vols.

A record of each birth in Allen County listing name, date of birth, place of birth, father's name, mother's maiden name, and address. Chronologically arranged. Handwritten. Volumes average 200 pages. 18 x 12 x 2.5. County courthouse. Room 206.

230. RECORD OF DEATHS
1867-1907. 2 vols.

Record of deaths in Allen County listing names, addresses, dates, and causes. Alphabetical index in front of each volume. Handwritten. Volumes average 200 pages. 18 x 12 x 2. County courthouse. Room 206.

231. MARRIAGE RECORD
1831—. 30 vols.

A record of marriages in Allen County listing names, addresses, and dates. Alphabetical index in front of each volume. Handwritten on printed forms. Volumes average 600 pages. 16 x 13 x 2.5. County courthouse. Room 206A.

232. RECORDS OF MARRIAGES
1852—. 60 file boxes.

Marriage licenses and records of marriages in Allen County. Cardex system. 13 x 9.5 x 5. County courthouse. Room 206A.

Record of Dependents

233. EPILEPTIC RECORD
1896-1911. 1 vol.

A record of admission of epileptics to state hospital listing name, address, date, and findings in each case. Alphabetical index in front of volume. Handwritten on printed forms. 200 pages. 18 x 12 x 2. County courthouse. Room 206.

234. LUNACY RECORD
1881—. 9 vols.

A record of each commitment to the asylum listing name, address, and date. Alphabetical index in front of each volume. Handwritten on printed forms. Volumes average 600 pages. 18 x 12 x 2.5. County courthouse. Room 206.

235. RECORD OF FEEBLE-MINDED YOUTH
1905-1914. 1 vol.

Record of commitment of feeble-minded children in the state institution for feeble-minded, listing each child's name, parents name, addresses, and dates. Alphabetical index in front of volume. Handwritten on printed forms. 200 pages. 18 x 12 x 1.5. County courthouse. Room 206.

236. LUNACY, EPILEPTIC, FEEBLE- MINDED, DEAF AND DUMB, AND WITNESS DOCKET
1907-1925. 4 vols.
A record of cases of lunatics, epileptics, feeble-minded, deaf and dumb, Listing names, dates, findings, and other facts about each case. Alphabetical index in front of each volume. Handwritten. Volumes average 350 pages. 18 x 13 x 2. County courthouse. Room 206.

237. REGISTER OF BLIND
1904-1907. 1 vol.
A record listing name and address of blind persons in Allen County. No index. Handwritten. 120 pages. 14 x 8 x 1. County courthouse. Room 206.

Juvenile Court

238. RECORD OF UNOFFICIAL CASES
1914—. 32 file boxes.
Records of unofficial cases of boys and girls and some records of mothers' pensions listing names, case number, and dates. Cardex system. 25 x 16 x 11 and 14 x 11 x 5. County courthouse. Room 104.

239. JUVENILE COURT CASES
1906-1929. 90 file boxes.
Records and original papers pertaining to cases tried in juvenile court listing names, dates, and findings. Cardex system. 11 x 10.5 x 5. County courthouse. Room 108V.

240. JUVENILE COURT JOURNAL
1906—. 7 vols.
Record of juvenile cases before probate court of Allen County listing names, case numbers, and findings. Alphabetical index in front of each volume. Handwritten on printed forms. Volumes average 300 pages. 18 x 12 x 1.5. County courthouse. Room 104.

241. JUVENILE COURT DOCKET
1906—. 8 vols.
Record of the nature and disposition of cases brought before juvenile court listing names, dates, case numbers, and findings. Alphabetical index in front of each

volume. Handwritten on printed forms. Volumes average 300 pages. 18 x 12 x 1.5. County courthouse. Room 104.

242. MOTHERS' PENSION JOURNAL
1914—. 1 vol.

Record of confirming and allowing the application for mothers' pensions listing names, addresses, dates, and amounts. Alphabetical index in front of volume. Typed. 500 pages. 16 x 11 x 2.5. County courthouse. Room 104.

243. MOTHERS' PENSION DOCKET AND RECORD
1914-1934. 2 vols.

Record of each application for mothers' pension listing name, date, number of children, and remarks. Alphabetical index in front of each volume. Typed. Volumes average 600 pages. 18 x 12 x 2.5. County courthouse. Room 104.

The county prosecutor, unlike the sheriff and coroner, is relatively one of the newer agencies in the administration of criminal justice. This office, established in America by the English during the colonial period, offers a striking difference in the development of American criminal procedures in contrast to the English where criminal prosecutions, in the main, were instituted by private persons. As developed and recent years, the office of the prosecutor has become one of the state's most important agencies in its defense against modern crime.

The acts of the Northwest territory place the responsibility for criminal prosecutions upon the attorney-general, who, in turn, appointed and commissioned persons to prosecute cases in the respective counties.

While the acts of Northwest territory outlined the local institutions for the newer states, the constitution of Ohio contained no provisions for a prosecutor leaving its creation to the discretion of the legislature. In 1803 during the first session of the legislature, an act was passed authorizing the supreme court to appoint in each county of the state an attorney to prosecute cases in behalf of the state. (1 O.L. 50.) Two years later the appointing power was vested in the court of common pleas. (3 O.L. 47.) The office remained an appointive one until 1833 when the electorate of the county were directed to elect a prosecutor in each county for a two-year term. (Chase., *op., cit.*, III, 1935; JR. Swan, *Statutes of the State of Ohio*, Columbus, 1841, 737.) The act of 1852 left the office elective and the term unchanged. In 1881 the term of office was set at three years, but it was reduced to two years in 1906. (78 O.L. 260; 96 O.L. 271-272.

Under the present system the prosecutor is elected for a four year term. He is required to give bond of not less than one thousand dollars conditioned for the faithful performance of the duties of his office. In the event the office becomes vacant the court of common pleas is authorized to appoint a successor. In the case of disability the office is filled by an appointment by the county commissioners. (G.C. sec. 2, 912.)

The county prosecutor is authorized to appoint clerks, assistants, and stenographers and set their salaries. Since 1911, he has been authorized to appoint a secret service agent or officer whose duty it is to aid him in the collection of evidence to be used in the trial of criminal cases and in matters of a criminal nature. The compensation of such an officer is determined by the court of common pleas. (G.C. sec. 2, 914-2, 915.)

Most important among the duties of the prosecuting attorney are those connected with criminal prosecutions. These duties, differing little from the early days of the office, include the prosecution on behalf of the state of all complaints, suits, and controversies in which the state is a party, and such other suits, matters, and controversies as he is directed by law to prosecute within or without his county, in the probate court, court of common pleas, and court of appeals. In conjunction with the attorney-general, he prosecutes cases in the supreme court in his county. (G.C. sec. 2, 916.)

In felony cases, when a complaint is made to the prosecutor, he is required to examine the evidence and determine if it is sufficient for prosecution. If he decides in the affirmative, he prepares the evidence for presentation to the grand jury. If this body returns an indictment the prosecutor prepares to present the evidence in trial court. The court of common pleas may appoint an attorney to assist the prosecutor in criminal cases. (G.C. sec. 2, 925.) In the case of conviction, the prosecutor causes execution to be issued for the fines or cost and pays all moneys so received into the county treasury. (G.C. sec. 2, 916.)

Besides prosecution in criminal cases, the prosecutor also acts in civil matters. He may bring suit in the name of the state when he is convinced that public money is being misapplied or is being illegally withheld or withdrawn from the county treasury. Moreover, he may bring suit against persons violating the obligations of contracts at which the county is a party, or when county property is being used illegally or illegally occupied. (G.C. sec. 2, 921.)

In addition to these, other duties have been prescribed by statute. On the request of the judge of the juvenile court, he must prosecute individuals for committing crimes against children. (G.C. sec. 6, 212-5-7.) At the instigation of the secretary of state, he must prosecute any officer who refuses to furnish gratuitously statistical information for the use of that office. (G.C. sec. 174.)

The county prosecutor has also served in an advisory capacity since 1881. (78 O.L. 260.) He acts as an advisor to all county boards and officials and to township officers, who may require his opinion in writing on matters connected with their official duties. (G.C. sec. 2, 917.) In addition to this, he prepares official bonds for all county officers. (G.C. sec. 2, 920.)

The prosecuting attorney is required to make annually a report to the county commissioners stating the number of criminal prosecutions completed, the name or names of the party or parties to each, and the amount collected in fines, costs, and the amount forfeited. (G.C. sec. 2, 925.) Moreover on the demand of the attorney-general he must make an annual report on all criminal actions prosecuted by indictment in his county, on forms provided by the state. (G.C. sec. 2, 925; 78 O.L. 120; 90 O.L. 225.)

244. MISCELLANEOUS

1935—. 1 file box.

Records of non-support cases, reports on injuries listing names and case numbers. (Official records for this office are taking care of through office of clerk of courts.) No index. 23 x 11 x 5.5. L.T.B., Suite 100B, north room.

The office of county sheriff, one of the oldest elective offices in America, had its inception in the Anglo-Saxon period of English history. (George Burton Adams, *Constitutional History of England*, New York, 1921, 17-19; W.A. Morris, "The Office of Sheriff in the Anglo-Saxon Period," *English Historical Review*, XXXI, 19-40.) As developed during the Anglo-Norman state, the sheriff, as the king's representative in the shire was empowered to collect taxes, conduct court, preserve order, and defend and protect the king's interest and prerogatives. But the arbitrary exercise of such extensive powers, together with the development of better methods of administration during the thirteenth and throughout the centuries which followed results in a gradual reduction of his duties. At the beginning of the seventeenth century, although the sheriff continued to hold court in the shire for minor cases and presided at the sessions of the shire court for the election of members to parliament, he was in other respects little more than an executive agent of the courts bound to summon juries, execute judgments of the court, and administer the county jail. (Adams, *op. ct.*, 58, 87, 91. See also C.H. Haskins. *Norman Institutions, Harvard Historical Studies*, XXIV, 46.)

The ancient institution, in modified form, was introduced in the American colonies; and as was natural, was continued by the status following independence. (For a comparative study of the sheriff in England and the Chesapeake colonies, see Cyrus Harold Korraker, The Seventeenth-Century Sheriff, Chapel Hill, 1930.) The office took on a new significance, when, in the latter part of the eighteenth century, a flood of colonists swept across the Alleghenies to establish homes in the Northwest Territory, as organized by congress in 1787. In the remoter west the pioneers, far removed from the orderly legal processes and courts of the east, was subjected to the machinations of a lawless element, as evidenced in every new community. In 1792 the governor and judges of the territory adopted an act which provided for the appointment, by the governor, of a sheriff in each county, and defined his duties. The sheriff was directed to keep and preserve the peace, suppress affrays, routs, riots, unlawful assemblies and insurrections; he was bound to apprehend, and confine in jail all felons and traitors; he was to return persons, who, after having committed a crime in his county, had taken refuge in another. In addition to this, he was directed to attend upon the court of common pleas and the court of appeals during the sessions, and, when directed, execute all warrants, writs, and processes to him directly by the proper and lawful authority. (Pease, *op. cit.*, I, 8.)

Ohio entered the union as a state in 1803. The office of sheriff was continued by constitutional provision, and was made elective for a two-year term.

(*Ohio Const. 1802*, Art. V, sec. I.) The constitution of 1851, although not specifically providing for the office, stated that no person shall be eligible to the office for more than four in any period of six years. (*Ohio Const. 1851*, Art. X, sec. 3.) The term of office remained at two years until 1936 when it was extended to four years. (116 O.L. pt. 2, 1st sess. H. 603.) The sheriff received his remuneration from fees, and not until 1906 was a definite salary specified by legislature. (3 O.L. 49-51; 33 O.L. 18; 35 O.L. 53; 52 O.L. 86; 98 O.L. 95.)

The duties of the sheriff were, and are, prescribed by statute. During the legislative session of 1805 the general assembly passed an act defining the duties of the sheriff, which, in all respects, was similar to the provision inherited from the territorial code. (3 O.L. 156-38.) In the same year the sheriff was designated as the county's executioner, and was bound to carry out sentences of death as imposed by the courts upon those convicted of murder. Hanging was the legal method adopted for the infliction of the death penalty. (Salmon P. Chase, *The Statutes of Ohio*, 3 vols., Cincinnati, 1833-1835, I, 97-101; 109, 442-443.) Public executions, the general rule during the earlier years, were abolished in 1844. (42 O.L. 71.)

As in England the sheriff, during the earlier years of his office, was required to notify the electors of his county of the time and place of holding elections. He was required to furnish, at the expense of the county, ballot boxes; he was required to hold special elections when so directed by the governor; and given the duty of delivering the poll books to the secretary of state. (2 O.L. 88-89; 3 O.L. 331-332.)

An act of 1824, repealing the act of 1805, redefined the duties of the sheriff as a conservator of the peace in his county and as an executive agent of the courts. (29 O.L. 112.) The present duties of the sheriff in this respect are survivals from the provisions of this act. (29 O.L. 112-113; 82 O.L. 26.) In the execution of his duties, as prescribed by law, he was empowered to summon to his aid such persons as he deemed necessary to perform his lawful duty. (29 O.L. 112-113.) Thus the *posso comitatus* was at his disposal as it is today. Six years earlier, in 1818, the sheriff was authorized to appoint, with the consent of the court of common pleas, one or more deputies, who, like himself, were required to give bond for the faithful performance of the duties of their office. The sheriff was made responsible for their neglect of duty or misconduct in office. (29 O.L. 410.)

Not only was the sheriff charged with the duty of apprehending law violators, but he was made responsible for their safe keeping. As early as 1803 he was made official custodian of the county jail. (3 O.L. 157.) Although the early statutes directed by the county commissioners to provide dungeons for the incarceration of prisoners, the act of 1847 directed the sheriff to exercise reasonable care for the preservation of the life, health, and welfare of those committed to his care. Indeed he was, and is, authorized to transport prisoners to other counties for safekeeping. (3 O.L. 157; 29 O.L. 112-113; 93 O.L. 131.) In 1910 provision was made for the removal of the sheriff by the governor if he were proved guilty of negligence in affording a prisoner adequate protection from mob violence. (101 O.L. 109.)

Although the sheriff is still regarded as the chief peace officer in the county, many of these earlier duties in this respect have been absorbed by the development of other agencies of law enforcement, notably the state highway patrol. On the other hand, the powers of the sheriff to suppress affrays, riots, and unlawful assemblies became especially important in times of strikes or threatened riots. The sheriff, too, may arrest on a properly issued warrant any person charged with the probability of doing injury to another person or the property of another. (G.C. sec. 13,463.) Moreover, since 1910 the sheriff has forwarded to the bureau of criminal identification all fingerprints of persons arrested for any felony (110 O.L. 5; 109 O.L.585.), and since 1913 has been authorized to arrest any prisoner violating his parole. (103 O.L. 405.)

As an executive agent of the court the sheriff still executes all writs, warrants, and other processes directed to him by lawful authority; he attends the court of common pleas and court of appeals during their sessions, and, when required upon the probate court. (29 O.L. 112; 316; 82 O.L. 26; 103 O.L. 405.)

Other historical functions of the sheriff have been altered or abolished. His duties regarding the announcement of elections long since have been taken over by the county boards of elections. His duties regarding executions were absorbed by the state in 1886. (83 O.L. 145.) Although the jury commission has supplanted the clerk of courts in the matter of selecting names of prospective jurors from the jury wheel, the sheriff's duties in this respect remain much as they were in the earlier years of his office.

The sheriff was, and is, required by law to keep a record of the business of his office. The present practice of keeping a foreign execution docket began in 1838. (36 O.L. 18; 57 O.L. 6; 84 O.L. 208-209.) Since 1843 the sheriff has kept a jail register (41 O.L. 74.), and since 1868 a cash book. (65 O.L. 115; 84 O.L. 208; 86 O.L. 239.) Indexes, direct and reverse to the foreign execution docket, were prescribed by the legislature in 1925. (111 O.L. 31.) Since 1843 the sheriff has been required, on the first Monday of September in each year, to submit to the county commissioners a certified statement of all fines and costs collected during the year and the amount of fees collected and paid to the clerk of courts of common pleas.

(G.C. sec. 2. 504; 41 O.L.66; 48 O.L.66.) Moreover, since 1843 he has been required to transmit annually the jail register, in certified copies, to the clerk of courts, county auditor, and the secretary of state. (41 O.L. 74.)

The sheriff's records, public property and open to the inspection of the public, are transferred together with all effects apportaining to the office, to his successor.

Cash Books, Ledgers, and Registers

245. CASH BOOKS

1859—. 17 vols. (1882-1894, missing.)

Record of cash collections listing dates, names, and amounts. Alphabetical index in front of each volume. Handwritten. Volumes average 300 pages. 18 x 13 x 2.5. County courthouse.

1859-1865, 1868, 2 volumes. Room 400B.
1866-1867, 1882, 1894, 1896-1906, 1910—, 13 volumes. Room 207.
1907-1910, 2 volumes. Room 400A.

246. SHERIFF'S RECORD OF FEES

1892—. 14 vols.

A record listing amount of fees, title of case, and by whom paid. Alphabetical index in front of each volume. Handwritten. Volumes average 300 pages. 18 x 12 x 2. County courthouse.

1892-1897, 1902-1907, 2 volumes. Room 400B.
1898-1901, 1907—, 12 volumes. Room 207.

247. LEDGER

1870-1905. 2 vols. (1871-1903, missing.)

Ledger postings of accounts listing names, dates, and amounts. No index. Handwritten. Volumes average 100 pages. 13 x 8 x 1.5. County courthouse. Room 207.

248. UNCLAIMED COST AND OTHER MONEYS PAID TO COUNTY

1919-1927. 1 vol.

Record of unclaimed cost and other moneys paid to county listing dates and amounts. Chronologically arranged. Handwritten. 150 pages. 16 x 12 x 1.5. County courthouse. Room 207.

249. BOARD BILLS
1898-1902. 1 file box.

A record of jail board bills, listing amounts and dates. Cardex system. 5 x 10 x 15. County courthouse. Room 207.

250. INSURANCE POLICY REGISTER
1880-1883. 1 vol.

A record of insurance listing number of each policy, name of company, and amount of insurance. Chronologically arranged. Handwritten. 100 pages. 16 x 9 x 1.5. County courthouse. Room 207.

Dockets

251. FOREIGN EXECUTION DOCKETS
1877—. 5 vols.

Record of judgments listing name of owner of property, address, date, and writ. Alphabetical indexed in front of each volume. 1877-1916, handwritten; 1916—. Typed. Volumes average 300 pages. 16 x 11 x 3. County courthouse.

1877-1897, 3 volumes. Room 400B.
1898—, 2 volumes. Room 207.

252. FOREIGN SUMMONS DOCKET
1883—. 8 vols. (1884-1911, missing.)

Record of summons for persons out of the county, listing name of each party, date, and case number. Alphabetical index in front of each volume. 1883, handwritten; 1911—. Typed. Volumes average 500 pages. 16 x 12 x 13. County courthouse.

1883, 1 volume. Room 400A.
1911-1913, 1916—, 6 volumes. Room 207.
1913-1915, 1 volume. Room 400B.

Court Orders

253. COURT ORDERS
1934—. 1 file box.

These are various orders issued by court to the sheriff. Cardex system. 5 x 10 x 15. County courthouse. Room 207.

254. EXECUTIONS
1935—. 1file box.
Record of sheriff's executions, listing names and dates. Cardex system. 5 x 10 x 15. County courthouse. Room 207.

255. MITTIMUS
1898—. 3 file boxes.
Warrants for commitments to prison each listing name and date. Cardex system. 5 x 10 x 15. County courthouse. Room 207.

256. RELEASES
1929-1931. 2 file boxes.
Orders of release of prisoners listing names and dates of releases. Cardex system. 5 x 10 x 15. County courthouse. Room 207.

257. SUBPOENAS
1936. 1 file box.
Issued subpoenas listing names, addresses, dates, and case numbers. Cardex system. 5 x 10 x 15. County courthouse. Room 207.

258. SUMMONS
1936. 1 file box.
Summons listing names, addresses, dates, and case numbers. Cardex system. 5 x 10 x 15. County courthouse. Room 207.

259. COPIES
1935—. 1 file box.
Record of court orders for summons listing name, address, date, and case number Cardex system. 5 x 10 x 15. County courthouse. Room 207.

260. Alphabetically FILE WARRANTS
1929—. 1 file box.
Warrants filed listing names and dates. Cardex system. 12 x 13 x 27. County courthouse. Room 207.

261. APPRAISEMENTS
1929—. 1 file box.
Record of appraisements of properties listing name of owner, description of property, and appraisal value. Cardex system. 5 x 10 x 15. County courthouse. Room 207.

262. RECORD OF SHERIFF'S SALES
1935—. 2 file boxes.
A record of sheriff's sales listing names, dates, and amounts. Cardex system. 5 x 10 x 15. Courthouse. Room 207.

Criminal Records

263. CRIMINAL'S DESCRIPTION
1931—. 1 file box.
Circulars of descriptions of criminals; also fingerprints. Cardex system. 12 x 13 x 3. County courthouse. Room 207.

264. MONTHLY COMPLAINT FILES
1931—. 1 file box.
Complaints received by sheriff listing names, dates, and complaints, Cardex system. 12 x 13 x 27. County courthouse. Room 207.

265. STOLEN AUTOS AND CRIMINAL PHOTOS
1935—. 1 file box.
Information on stolen cars listing names, addresses, and kind of cars; also photos of criminals listing names and description. Cardex system. 6 x 17 x 27. County courthouse. Room 207.

266. CHICKEN TATTOO IDENTIFICATION MAPS
1935—. 1 file box.
Record listing name of owner of chickens and tattoo registration number. Cardex system. 6 x 13 x 27. County courthouse. Room 207.

267. JAIL REGISTER

1860—. 8 vols. (1878-1893, 1896-1906, missing.)

Record of commitment and release of prisoners listing names, dates, of admittance and release. Chronologically arranged. Handwritten. Volumes average pages. 14 x 14 x 1. County courthouse.

1860-1970, 1895-1896, 1923—, 4 volumes. Room 207.

1870-1879, 1 volume. Room 400A.

1894-1895, 1907-1923, 3 volumes. Room 400B.

268. JUVENILE RECORD

1927. 1 vol.

100 blank stubs. 100 pages. 18 x 8 x 1.5. County courthouse. Room 207.

Miscellaneous

269. POLICEMAN'S RECORD OF STRAYS, ETC.

1864-1891. 1 vol.

A record of strays listing notices and dates of notices and name of owners when reported. Alphabetical index in front of volume. Handwritten. 500 pages. 12.5 x 8 x 1.5. County courthouse. Room 400B.

270. PARTITION RECORD

1881-1887. 1 vol.

A record of partitions listing names, addresses, dates, and remarks. Alphabetical index in front of volume. Handwritten. 160 pages. 16 x 12 x 2. County courthouse. Room 207.

271. NEWSPAPER CLIPPINGS

1935—. 1 vol.

These are various clippings from newspapers which have been pasted into volume. No index. 50 pages. 12 x 14 x 2. County courthouse. Room 207.

While the acts of the Northwest Territory outlined the local institutions of the newer states, the first constitution of Ohio contain no provision for the office of the county auditor, leaving its creation to the discretion of the legislature. It was not, however, until 1820 the general assembly by joint resolution appointed a county auditor in each county for a one-year term. (18 O.L. 70.) A year later the office became an elective one, and has so continued. (19 O.L. 116.) The term of office was fixed at one year in 1821, two years in 1831, and 3 years in 1877. (19 O.L. 116; 29 O.L. 280; 74 O.L.381.) The term remain at three years until 1906 when it was reduced to two years. (98 O.L. 273.) In 1919 the term of office was extended to four years. (108 O.L. pt. 2, 1294.)

During the early years of his office the auditor was required, as he is today, to take an oath, give bond for the faithful performance of the duties of this office, and transfer to his successor all books, records, maps, and other papers appertaining to his office. (19 O.L. 116; R.S. 1033; G.C. sec. 2,559; 2, 582.) He was required, also, to preserve in his office all copies of the entries, surveys, extracts, and other documents as may have been transmitted to his office from the auditor of state. (Chase., *op. cit.*, 1378.) The auditor was authorized to appoint deputies to aid him in the performance of his duties. He and his sureties were, and are, liable for the official acts of the subordinates. Since 1869, a record of such appointments have been filed with the county treasurer. (G.C. sec. 2,563; 66 O.L. 35.) If the office were to become vacant the county commissioners were, and are, authorized to appoint some suitable person to fill the vacancy. (29 O.L. 280-291; 67 O.L. 103.)

The first auditor in each county was required to list all lands subject to taxation lying within his county. From this list and a list submitted to him by the county commissioners and the state auditor, he was directed to make out a tax duplicate to be kept in a book for that purpose. After completing the duplicate, he turned it over to the "tax collector," who, in turn, proceeded to demand payment. (18 O.L. 70.) Moreover the auditor was directed to make a list from the treasurer's duplicate of all lands on which taxes were delinquent. And the event such lands were "sold for taxes" the auditor was authorized to grant a deed to the purchaser. (18 O.L. 70; 19 O.L. 116.) Subsequent legislation expanded and itemized the duties of the auditor regarding taxation. During the decade of the forties the offices of county assessors were abolished and provision was made for township assessors whose duty it was to list all taxable property in the township and make a return to the auditor. (39 O.L. 22-25.) Since 1874 the auditor has been required, by statute, to keep a book in which he lists additions to and deductions from the amount of the tax assessment. (71 O.L. 30.) The auditor's duties regarding taxation have, with modifications to meet modern requirements, continued much as they were during the earlier years of the office.

The county auditor, along with the county treasurer and county prosecutor, has served as a member of the county budget commission. As secretary to this body he is required to keep full and accurate records of the proceedings of the board. For the purpose of adjusting the tax rates and fixing the amount to be levied each year, the commissioners are governed by the amount of taxable property as shown on the auditors tax list for the current year. The auditor submits to the commissioners the annual tax budget submitted to him by each taxing authority of each subdivision together with an estimate prepared by the auditor of the state, of the amount of any state levy, and other information as the budget commission may request or the state tax commission may require. (G.C. sec. 5, 626-19; 112 O.L. 339.)

Another important function of the county auditor has been the examination and approval of bills and other claims against the county before payment. Since 1831 the auditor has been authorized to issue all warrants on the county treasurer for monies payable from the county treasurer, upon the presentation of the proper voucher, and has been required to preserve all warrants showing the number, date of issue, amount for which drawn, and whose favor, and for what purpose and on what fund. (G.C. sec. 2, 570; R.S. 1024; 29 O.L. 280-291; 67 O.L. 103.) Money due to the state is paid on warrant of the auditor of state. (*Ibid.*, sec. 1, 024.) Since 1904 a bill or voucher for payment of any fund controlled by the county commissioners has been filed with a county auditor and entered in a book for that purpose at least five days before its approval for payment by the commissioners. When approved the date thereof is entered in such a book opposite the claim. (97 O.L. 25; 408 O.L. pt. 1, 266-272.)

Besides approving bills and claims against the county, the auditor was early given the duty of certifying all moneys, except collections on the tax duplicate, into the county treasurer, specifying by whom paid and the fund to which such payment is credited. Such money he charges to the treasurer and keeps a duplicate in his office. Since 1835 all costs collected in penitentiary cases which have been paid by the state or which are to be so paid, have been certified into the treasury as belonging to the state. (33 O.L. 44; 67 O.L. 103.)

The auditor, since 1831, has kept an account current with the county treasurer showing the payments of money into the treasury listing the time, by whom paid and from what fund. Upon receiving the treasurer's daily statement he was, and is, directed to enter on his account current as a charge to the treasurer the amount shown. (29 O.L. 280-291; 67 O.L. 103.)

In 1902 the legislature made provision for a system of uniform accounting and auditing for all public offices, under the director of a bureau of inspection in the auditor of state's office. The act provided, also, for the annual examination of the finances of all public offices. (95 O.L. 511-515.) Since 1904 liquor taxes, cigarette taxes, and inheritance taxes have constituted separate funds. All other taxes are credited to the general fund. (97 O.L. 453.) Semi-annually the auditor makes a settlement with the treasurer ascertaining the amount of taxes the treasurer is to "stand charged." Semi-annual settlements began in 1881; previous to that time settlements had been made annually. G.C. sec. 2, 596; 56 O.L. 128; 78 O.L. 226.)

Since 1904 the auditor has been required to report to the commissioners on the state of county finances. On the first business day of each month the auditor prepares, in duplicate, a statement of the finances of the county for the proceeding month. After comparing it with the treasurer's balances, the statement is submitted to the commissioners, who, in turn, post one copy of it in the auditor's office where it remains for at least thirty days for the inspection and examination of the public. (67 O.L. 103; 97 O.L. 457.)

During the development of the office other duties have been conferred upon the auditor with great diversity. For example, since 1833 he has been authorized to discharge from imprisonment, any person confined in jail for the non-payment of any fine or amercement due to the county, when, in his opinion, the fine appears to be uncollectible. (G.C. sec. 2, 576; 31 O.L. 18; 67 O.L. 103.)

The present-day duty of reporting to the auditor of state statistics of deaf, dumb, blind, insane, and idiotic persons in his county with the names and post office address of their parents or guardians, had its beginning in 1861. (58 O.L. 40.) Eight years later saw the beginning of the practice of reporting to the same officer statistics of livestock in his county, as returned to his office by assessors, and by abstract of the funded and unfunded indebtedness of his county, and of each township, city, village, and school district. (G.C. sec. 2, 604.) During the same year, 1861, the auditor was given his present day duty of issuing peddlers' licenses to persons who filed a statement of his stock and trade and conformity with the law requiring the listing of such stock for taxation, and since 1917 he has issued dog licenses. (59 O.L. 67; 79 O.L.96; 107 O.L. 34.)

Besides his own duties, of which an incomplete account has been given, the auditor was early given the duty as serving as clerk to the county commissioner. He was, and is, required to keep an accurate record of their proceedings and preserve all documents, books, records, maps, and papers which might be required to be filed in his office. (G.C. sec. 2, 566; 67 O.L. 103.) Moreover, since 1850 he has been the official custodian of the reports submitted to the commissioners by the prosecuting attorney, the clerk of courts, the sheriff, and the treasurer. These reports have been recorded by the auditor and books kept especially for that purpose. (G.C. sec. 2, 504; R.S. 886; 48 O.L. 66.)

Then, too, since 1861, the auditor has served as the sealer of weights and measures, and is responsible for the preservation of the copies of the original standards delivered to his office. He enforces all state laws regulating weights and measures in is county. (G.C. sec. 2, 615; 58 O.L. 78; 101 O.L. 234.)

In recent years there has been much criticism of the auditor's office. The chief complaint is, of course, that there is a duplication of work in the auditors and in the treasurer's offices. The daily registers are, in all respects, similar.

Budget Commission

With the increased expenditures, following the World War, the need for improved methods of county finance administration became greater. This need was met, in 1927, by the establishment of a budget commission in each county. This commission, consisting of the county auditor, county treasurer, and the prosecuting attorney, receives and examines the annual budget of the county, municipal, township and school authorities, with an estimate of the amount to be raised, for the state purposes in each subdivision. (112 O.L. 399.) If the total amount exceeds the amount authorized to be raised, the commission adjusts the amount to be raised, and may change and revise the estimates. The commission may reduce all items in the budget, but is prohibited from increasing the total of any budget or any item.

The adjusted budget is certified to the taxing authority in each subdivision. If the work of the commission is satisfactory, each taxing authority by ordinance or resolution authorizes the necessary tax levies and certifies them to the county auditor. (G.C. sec. 5, 625-25.) On the other hand, the taxing authority in any subdivision may, through its fiscal officer, appeal from the decision of the budget commission to the state tax commission of Ohio which is empowered to adjust the estimates of revenues and balances in fixing the tax rate. (G.C. sec. 5, 625-628.)

Tax Assessments and Appraisements

272. ASSESSMENT BOOK

1844-1932. 252 vols. (1846-1858, 1860-1869, 1871-1879, 1881-1886, 1888-1895, 1897-1909, 1911-1912, 1916-1923, 1925, 1927-1930, missing.)

A record listing name of owner, description of each property, value and assessment. No index. 1844-1908, handwritten; 1908-1932, typed. Volumes average 175 pages. 19 x 14.5 x 1.25. County courthouse.

1844-1845, 1859, 56 volumes. Room 202.
1913-1915. 69 volumes. Room 400B.
1926, 1931-1932, 127 volumes. Room 102.

273. SPECIAL ASSESSMENT RECORD

1903. 1 vol.

A record listing owner's name, purpose of assessment, and amount. No index. Handwritten. 120 pages. 15 x 12 x 1. County courthouse. Room 202.

274. ADDITIONS AND DEDUCTIONS

1878—. 9 vols.

A record listing additions to and deductions from tax list. (Prior to 1925 Allen County and city of Lima were in the same volume. Since 1925 they are in separate volumes.) Indexed as to wards and school districts. Handwritten. Volumes average 250 pages. 18 x 12 x 2.5. County courthouse.

1878-1892, 1925—, 5 volumes. Room 202.
1892-1899, 1821-1825, 2 volumes. Room 400.
1900-1913, 1 volume. Room 400B.
1914-1921, 1 volume. Room 102.

275. BOOK OF ADDITIONS

1923—. 8 vols.

A duplicate of auditor's additions to tax list listing names and amounts. No index. Handwritten on printed forms. Volumes average 300 pages. 16 x 14 x 2.5. County courthouse.

1924-1927, 1929-1931, 3 volumes. Room 102.
1923-1924, 1927-1929, 1931—, 4 volumes. Room 202.
1934-1935, 1 volume. Room 100.

276. RE-APPRAISEMENTS

1890-1900. 8 vols.

A record of re-appraisements and assessments of property and taxing districts of Allen County listing name of owner, description of property, and amount of assessment. No index. Handwritten on printed forms. Volumes average 25 pages. 16 x 11 x .5. County courthouse. Room 102.

277. QUADRENNIAL APPRAISEMENT, CITY OF LIMA

1910-1911. 1 vol. (— 1910. Missing.)

A record listing name of owner, lot number, and equalization. Alphabetical index in front of volume. Handwritten. 250 pages. 18 x 12 x 2. County courthouse. Room 102.

278. RECORD OF RAILROAD APPRAISEMENTS

1903-1910. 2 vols.

A record of proceedings of railroad board of appraisers and assessors. No index. Handwritten. Volumes average 150 pages. 18 x 13 x 2. County courthouse. Room 202.

Tax Duplicates

279. AUDITOR'S DUPLICATE

1830-1933. 350 vols. (1831-1833, 1835-1840, 1843, 1848, 1850, 1852, 1921, missing.)

A record listing each owner's name, description of property, general tax, road tax, and total tax. Some are alphabetically arranged as to names of owners. 1830-1908, handwritten; 1908-1935, typed. Volumes average 300 pages. 20 x 14 x 2.5. County courthouse.

1830, 1856, 1913, 1920, 16 volumes. Room 400B.

1923, 1931, 8 volumes. Room 102.

1935, 3 volumes. Room 100.

1830, 1855, 1857-1912, 1914-1919, 1922, 1924-1930, 1932-1934, 325 volumes. Room 202.

280. TREASURERS' DUPLICATE
1860. 1 vol.
A record listing each owner's name, description of property, and amounts. No index. Handwritten. 400 pages. 18 x 12 x 2. County courthouse. Room 202.

281. AUDITOR'S LIST OF DUPLICATE
1882-1922 4 vols.
A record of each liquor license listing name of dealer, name of owner of property, description of property, and amount of fee. No index. Handwritten on printed forms. Volumes average 100 pages. 19 x 18 x 1. County courthouse.
1882-1885, 1906-1920, 2 volumes. Room 202.
1886-1894, 1 volume. Room 400B.
1903-1904, 1 volume. Room 102.

282. AUDITOR'S CIGARETTE DUPLICATE
1894-1931. 4 vols.
A record listing names of persons engaged in cigarette traffic, location of each property, name of owner of real estate, and record of assessment. No index. Handwritten. Volumes average 75 pages. 19 x 12 x 1. County courthouse.
1894-1918, 1906-1920, 2 volumes. Room 202.
1886-1894, 1 volume. Room 400B.
1903-1904, 1 volume. Room 102.

283. TREASURER'S CIGARETTE DUPLICATE, 1920-1930. 1 vol.
Record listing name of dealers, name of property owner, and location of building. No index. Handwritten. 60 pages. 18 x 12 x .5. County courthouse. Room 202.

284. IMPROVED HIGHWAY DUPLICATE
1915-1934. 4 vols. (1922-1924, missing.)
Highway duplicate listing road surveys, special assessments for highways, names, location, and amount of tax. Alphabetical index in front of each volume. Handwritten. Volumes average 200 pages. 16 x 11.5. x 1.25. County courthouse. Room 202.

285. SPECIAL DITCH DUPLICATE
1867—. 14 vols.

A duplicate giving a description of each ditch and cost of construction, description of property affected, and amount of tax. Alphabetical index in front of each volume. 1867-1898, handwritten; 1899—, handwritten on printed forms. Volumes average 200 pages. 16 x 12 x 1.5. County courthouse. Room 202.

286. PERSONAL TAX DUPLICATES
1932—. 40 file boxes.

Personal tax duplicates listing names, description of properties, and amount of tax. Cardex system. 27 x 16.75 x 11.5. County courthouse. Room 102, and steel file cabinet.

Tax Lists

287. AUDITOR'S LIST OF TAXES ON PERSONAL PROPERTY
1922-1931. 3 vols. (1926-1930 missing.)

A record listing evaluation of personal property, name, date, amount of tax, and penalty. Chronologically arranged. Typed. 2 volumes average 42 pages. 19 x 13 x .5. County courthouse.

1922-1925, 2 volumes. Room 202.
1931—, 1 volume. Room 102.

288. AUDITOR'S LIST EXEMPTED REAL AND PERSONAL PROPERTY
1922-1932. 1 vol.

A record giving name of owner, description of property, and value. No index. Typed. 150 pages. 17 x 14 x 1. County courthouse. Room 202.

289. AUDITOR'S TAX LIST
1935—. 4 file boxes.

Auditor's tax list listing name and amount of tax. Cardex system. 24 x 13 x 11.5. County courthouse. Room 202, in steel cabinets.

290. RECORD OF TRANSFERS
1869-1935. 20 vols.
A record of realty transfers listing to whom, from whom, amount, and description of property. Alphabetical index in front of each volume. Handwritten. Volumes average 300 pages. 18 x 12 x 3. County courthouse.
1875-1883, 1 volume. Room 102.
1912-1916, 1919-1921, 5 volumes. Room 400B.
1869-1874, 1882-1911, 1917-1918, 1922-1935, 14 volumes. Room 202.

291. TAX MAP SHEETS
1924. 1 vol.
A record listing names of owners and location of properties in city of Lima. Indexed as to wards and additions. Typed. 400 pages. 2 x 13 x 1.5. County courthouse. Room 202.

Tax Returns

292. ALLEN COUNTY RECORD OF LEVIES
1879. 1 vol.
A record listing rates of taxation for the different taxing districts in the county. No index. Handwritten. 100 pages. 18 x 11 x .5. County courthouse. Room 102.

293. BANK RETURNS FOR 1928
1 vol.
Tax notices for state banks for 1928 listing resources and liabilities. No index. Handwritten on printed forms. 25 pages. 15 x 8 x .5. County courthouse. Room 102.

294. INCORPORATED COMPANIES, RAILROADS, BANKS, ETC.
1914-1915. 1 vol.
A record listing tax returns of incorporated companies. Alphabetically arranged as to names of companies. 200 pages. 16 x 12 x 1.5. County courthouse. Room 202.

295. INHERITANCE TAX RECORD
1923-1924. 2 vols.
A record listing name of each administrator, executor, direct inheritance, and the inheritance tax. (One volume blank.) No index. Typed. 200 pages. 14 x 12 x 1.5. County courthouse.
1 blank volume. Room 400B.

1923-1924, 1 volume. Room 202.

296. OIL RETURNS FOR 1928

1 vol.

A record of returns of oil and gas properties listing name of each owner, name of each operator, giving description of properties, and amounts of oil or gas. No index. Handwritten on printed forms. 160 pages. 15 x 8 x .5. County courthouse. Room 102.

297. PERSONAL TAX RETURNS

1932-1935. 23 file boxes.

Filed record of personal tax returns. Cardex system. 11 x 17 x 26. County courthouse.

1932-1934, 15 paper file boxes. Room 102.

1932-1935, 8 file boxes. Room 100.

298. DAY BOOK, 1832-1842. 1 vol.

A record of taxes for schools and other purposes listing taxes, delinquents, fines and licenses. No index. Handwritten. 150 pages. 12 x 8 x 1.5. County courthouse. Room 202.

299. BOOK OF REMITTERS

1923-1935. 15 vols.

Stubs and carbon copies of auditor's remitters of taxes paid listing names, and amounts. No index. Handwritten on printed forms. Volumes average 200 pages. 16 x 14 x 2.5. County courthouse.

1923-1932, 11 volumes. Room 102.

1932-1934, 1 volume. Room 100.

1933-1935, 3 volumes. Room 102.

300. REFUNDERS

1883—. 1 vol.

A record listing name, chattel, and amount of each refund. No index. Handwritten. 300 pages. 16 x 12 x 1.5. County Courthouse Route 202.

301. RECORD OMITTED TAX CASES
1881-1892. 1 vol.

Auditor's record of meetings with omitted tax cases. Alphabetical index in front of volume. Handwritten. 320 pages. 16 x 12 x 2. County courthouse. Room 202.

302. SETTLEMENT RECORDS
1883-1923. 406 file boxes.

Tax settlement records listing names, dates, and amounts. Cardex system. File boxes average 13.5 x 10.75 x 5. County courthouse. Room 202, in steel cabinet.

303. ABSTRACT RECORD
1879-1881. 1 vol.

A record containing a settlement sheet listing name of township, state tax, county tax, poor tax, bridge tax, building tax, with the amount of each. No index. Handwritten on printed forms. 100 pages. 18 x 13 x 1.25. County courthouse. Room 102.

Delinquent Taxes

304. AUDITOR'S RECORD OF DELINQUENT TAXES AND ASSESSMENTS
1905—. 12 vols.

A record listing each delinquent owner's name, description of property, and amount of tax. No index. Indiscriminately handwritten and typed on printed forms. Volumes average 200 pages. 18 x 12 x 2, and 700 pages 12 x 10 x 4. County courthouse.

1905-1932, 8 volumes. Room 102.
1933-1934, 1 volume. Room 100.
1935—, 3 volumes. Room 202.

305. DELINQUENT BOOK
1833-1928. 16 vols.

A record listing each delinquent owner's name, description of property, value, and remarks. No index. 1833-1908 handwritten; 1908-1928, typed. Volumes average 400 pages. 14 x 12 x 2. County courthouse.

1833-1913, 1916-1928, 15 volumes. Room 202.
1914-1915, 1 volume. Room 102.

306. REDEMPTION CERTIFICATE

1921-1932, 3 vols. (— 1921 missing.)

Auditor's duplicate of certificates of redemption giving names and description of properties. No index. Handwritten on printed forms. Volumes average 200 pages. 16 x 7 x 1. County courthouse.

1921-1930, 1 volume. Room 102.

1923-1932, 2 volumes. Room 202.

307. QUADRENNIAL CERTIFICATE OF UNREDEEMED DELINQUENT LAND

1922-1930. 2 vols. (1926, missing.)

A record of unredeemed delinquent land listing name, description, and taxes. No index. 1922-1924, handwritten; 1930, typed. Volumes average 550 pages. 17 x 13.5 x 3. County courthouse.

1922-1924, 1 volume 202.

1930, 1 volume. Room 102.

308. DELINQUENT SALES

1863-1905. 5 vols. (— 1863, missing.)

Record listing owner's name, description of property, and the tax. No index. Handwritten. Volumes average 400 pages. 18 x 13 x 2. County courthouse. Room 202.

309. FORFEITED LAND SALES

1857-1915. 1 vol.

Record of forfeited lands listing description and sales of same. No index. Handwritten. 300 pages. 14 x 8 x 2. County courthouse. Room 202.

310. RECORD OF AUDITOR'S DEEDS

1895-1908. 1 vol.

Record of deeds by auditor for delinquent lands giving name and description of each property. Alphabetical index in front of volume. Handwritten. 150 pages. 14 x 11 x 2. County courthouse. Room 202.

311. DELINQUENT ADVERTISEMENTS
1874. 1 vol.
A record of advertisements of delinquents giving name and description of each property, value, and amount of tax. No index. Handwritten. 250 pages. 18 x 15 x 1.5. County courthouse. Room 202.

312. AUDITOR'S DUPLICATE DELINQUENT CHATTELS
1896-1903. 2 vols. (— 1896, missing.)
A duplicate of delinquent chattels in Lima and Allen County listing name of owner, valuation, and amount of tax. No index. Handwritten. Volumes average 250 pages. 16 x 12 x 1.5. County courthouse.
1896-1902, 1 volume. Room 102.
1903—, 1 volume. Room 202.

Bonds and Official Bonds

313. RECORD OF BONDS ISSUED
1881-1934. 3 vols. (1892-1907, missing.)
A record of bonds issued, listing names, amounts, interest, and coupons due. 1881-1892, no index; 1907-1934, alphabetical index in front of volume. Handwritten. Volumes average 160 pages. 15 x 12 x 2. County courthouse. Room 202.

314. RECORD OF OFFICIAL BOND
1831-1929. 3 vols. (1870-1884, missing.)
A record of bonds of county officials, listing name, address, office, and amount of each bond. Alphabetical index in front of each volume. Handwritten on printed forms. Volumes average 300 pages. 18 x 14 x 1.5. County courthouse.
1831-1869, 1914-1929, 2 volumes. Room 202.
1885-1914, 1 volume. Room 102.

315. BOND OF TAX OFFICERS
1915. 1 vol.
A record of bonds of assessors listing names, addresses, amounts, and dates. Alphabetical index in front of volume. Handwritten on printed forms. 228 pages. 16 x 11 x 1. County courthouse. Room 202.

Disbursements and Receipts

316. APPROPRIATION LEDGER

1925-1934. 9 vols.

A record listing name of payee, purpose, and amount paid. Chronologically arranged. Handwritten. Volumes average 400 pages. 14 x 12 x 3.5. County courthouse. Room 202.

317. LEDGER

1895-1926. 3 vols. (1912-1916, missing.)

A record of accounts of board of directors of Allen County infirmary. No index. Handwritten. Volumes average 250 pages. 17 x 16 x 1.5. County courthouse.

1895-1911, 2 volumes. Room 400B.

1917-1926, 1 volume. Room 202.

318. AUDITOR'S LEDGER

1904—. 15 vols.

A record of auditor's account with various funds, such as county relief, county treasurer, and undivided general tax. Alphabetical index in front of each volume. Handwritten. 500 pages. 18 x 12 x 2. County courthouse.

1904-1906, 1910-1935,13 volumes. Room 202.

1907-1909, 1 volume. Room 400B.

1936, 1 volume. Room 202B.

319. AUDITOR'S REGISTER

1871-1872. 1 vol.

A miscellaneous register of auditor's business transactions listing names and dates. No index. Handwritten. 100 pages. 23 x 16 x .75. County courthouse. Room 400B.

320. RECEIPTS JOURNAL

1926—. 11 vols.

A record listing names, purpose, and amount. Chronologically arranged. Handwritten. Volumes average 200 pages. 15 x 12 x 1. County courthouse. Room 202.

321. AUDITOR'S RECORD
1907—. 8 vols.

A record of various fees listing name by person whom paid, name of fund, amount, and date in each case. No index. Handwritten. Volumes average 300 pages. 16 x 12 x 2. County courthouse.

1907-1915, 4 volumes. Room 202.
1915-1927, 4 volumes. Room 400A.

322. RECORD
1926-1927. 1 vol.

A record of court fees listing name, case, date, and amount. Alphabetical index as to names of officials in front of volume. Handwritten. 200 pages. 14 x 9 x 1.5. County courthouse. Room 202.

323. SALARY RECORD
1915-1925. 1 vol.

A record listing name, date, and cost allowance for salaries. Chronologically arranged. Handwritten. 100 pages. 15 x 14 x 1. County courthouse. Room 102.

324. APPOINTMENTS AND SETTLEMENTS
1915-1926. 82 file boxes.

A record listing appointments and settlements of administrators and estates. Cardex system. File boxes average 16 x 10 x 4.50. County courthouse. Room 202, in steel cabinet.

325. SETTLEMENT RECORD
1883—. 5 vols.

General statements of treasurer's accounts and conditions of various funds. No index. Handwritten. Volumes average 100 pages. 30 x 15 x 1.5. County courthouse.

1883-1933, 4 volumes. Room 202.
1927—, 1 volume. Room 202A.

326. RECORD OF ORDERS
1866-1871. 2 vols.

A record of each order listing date, order number, to whom, for what, and the amount. No index. Handwritten. Volumes average 250 pages. 18 x 12 x 1.5. County courthouse. Room 102.

327. PAY-IN ORDERS

1915—. 26 vols. (1918-1924, 1927, missing.)

Duplicates of orders paid to treasurer of Allen County listing names of payors, dates, and amounts, No index. Handwritten on printed forms. Volumes average 250 pages. 12 x 11 x 1. County courthouse.

1915-1917, 1928-1930, 17 volumes. Room 202.

1925-1926, 1930-1932, 9 volumes. Room 102.

328. PAY-IN ORDERS

1929-1933. 3 file boxes.

Filed pay-in orders listing name, order number, date, and amount. Cardex system. 17 x 11.5 x 5. County courthouse. Room 202, in steel cabinet.

329. AUDITOR'S PAY-IN DOCKET

1923-1924. 1 vol. (— 1923. missing.)

Authority of auditor for treasurer to receive moneys listing names and amounts. No index. Handwritten. 200 pages. 14 x 9 x 1. County courthouse. Room 400B.

330. AUDITOR'S DOCKET OF BILLS FILED

1920-1927. 2 vols. (— 1920, missing.)

A record listing name, amount, date, and specific purpose of each bill. No index. Handwritten. 350 pages. 18 x 12 x 3. County courthouse. Room 102.

331. AUDITOR'S DOCKET, COMMISSIONER'S BILLS

1904—. 7 vols. (1921-1926, missing.)

A record listing date and number of each bill, name, amount, and specific purpose for which used. Indexed by separate volumes, see entry 332. Handwritten. Volumes average 200 pages. 18 x 12 x 1.5. County courthouse.

1904-1912, 1927-1932, 4 volumes. Room 102.

1912-1920, 1932—, 3 volumes. Room 202.

332. AUDITOR'S INDEX TO COMMISSIONERS' BILLS

1922—. 4 vols.

An index listing name, amount, and number of each bill. Handwritten. Volumes average 325 pages. 18 x 14 x 2.5. County courthouse.

1922-1925, 1931—, 2 volumes. Room 202.

1925-1930, 2 volumes. Room 102.

333. AUDITOR'S DOCKET, COUNTY HOME BILLS
1905—. 5 vols.

A record listing name, date, amount, and purpose of each bill filed. Indexed by separate volumes, see entry 334. Handwritten. Volumes average 300 pages. 18 x 12 x 2. County courthouse.

1905-1908, 1 volume. Room 400B.
1906—, 4 volumes. Room 202.

334. AUDITOR'S INDEX TO COUNTY HOME BILLS
1911—. 3 vols. (1927-1933 missing.)

An index to county home bills listing dates and amounts. Handwritten. Volumes average 500 pages. 18 x 16 x 2. County courthouse. Room 202.

335. HUMANE COST BILL RECORD, 1922-1927
1 vol. (— 1922, missing.)

A record listing names, amounts, and dates paid. No index. Handwritten. 300 pages. 18 x 14 x 1. County courthouse. Room 202.

336. INQUEST TO LUNACY COST BILL RECORD
1897-1906. 1 vol.

A record listing name of person on whom each inquest was held, name of person receiving fee, and the amount. No index. Handwritten. 320 pages. 18 x 12 x 2. County courthouse. Room 202.

337. CLERK'S VOUCHERS
1863-1919. 5 vols. (1902-1913, missing.)

A record of clerk's vouchers for county bills listing names and amounts. Alphabetical index in front of each volume. Handwritten. Volumes average 200 pages. 16 x 12 x 2. County courthouse.

1865-1895, 3 volumes. Room 202.
1896-1919, 2 volumes. Room 102.

338. PROBATE VOUCHER RECORD
1907-1922. 1 vol.

A record of certificates of fees of inspectors listing voucher number, amount, date, and name of person to whom issued in each case. Alphabetical index in front of volume. Typed. 200 pages. 16 x 11 x 1.5. County courthouse. Room 202.

339. VOUCHERS

1930—. 476 file boxes.

Auditor's vouchers listing dates, amounts, and use. Cardex system. 14 x 10.5 x 4. County courthouse. Room 202, in steel cabinet.

340. TREASURER'S WARRANTS

1882, 1903. 2 vols.

Auditor's duplicate of treasurer's warrants listing name, date, warrant number, and amount. No index. Handwritten on printed forms. Volumes average 250 pages. 13 x 9 x 2. County courthouse.

1882, 1 volume. Room 102.

1903, 1 volume. Room 202.

341. AUDITOR'S JOURNAL OF WARRANTS ISSUED AND PAYMENTS INTO TREASURY

1904—. 20 vols. (1919-1921, missing.)

Warrants issued by auditor listing name of party, purpose, and amount. No index. Handwritten. Volumes average 200 pages. 17 x 12 x 1.5. County courthouse.

1904-1934, 18 volumes. Room 202.

1934-1935, 1 volume. Room 202B.

1936, 1 volume. Room 202A.

342. AUDITOR'S COURT WARRANTS

1904—. 4 vols.

A record of court warrants issues listing names of parties, dates, and amounts. No index. Handwritten. Volumes average 200 pages. 18 x 12 x 2. County courthouse.

1904-1931, 3 volumes. Room 202.

1931—, 1 volume. Room 202A.

343. DIRECT HOUSING RELIEF WARRANTS

1935. 1 vol.

A record of warrants for direct housing relief presented for payment of taxes. No index. Handwritten. 250 pages. 12 x 11 x 1. County courthouse. Room 202A.

344. WARRANTS

1909—. 76 vols. (1920-1928, 1931-1932, missing.)

Stubs of auditor's warrants listing for each, name of party, amount, date, and fund. No index. Handwritten. Volumes average 300 pages. 17 x 14 x 2. Courthouse.

1909-1919, 38 volumes. Room 102.

1926—, 34 volumes. Room 202.

1936, 4 volumes. Room 202B.

Financial Reports

345. AUDITOR'S FINANCIAL REPORT

1872-1923. 19 vols. (1874-1878, 1887, 1895, 1897-1899, 1901-1908, 1913-1919, missing.)

A record of various accounts, allotments for distribution and money accounts, listing names, dates, amounts, and uses. Chronologically arranged. Indexed by separate volumes, see entry 340. Handwritten. Volumes average 100 pages. 16 x 14 x 1. County courthouse.

1872-1900, 1908-1920, 1922-1923, 17 volumes. Room 400B.

1910-1911, 1 volume. Room 102.

1920-1921, 1 volume. Room 202.

346. INDEX TO AUDITOR'S FINANCIAL REPORT

1913-1924. 3 vols. (1917-1920 missing.)

A detailed account of general funds for county purposes, listing names, dates, and amounts. Handwritten. Volumes average 150 pages. 17 x 14 x 1. County courthouse.

1913-1916, 1 volume. Room 102.

1921-1924, 2 volumes. Room 202.

347. RECORD OF EXAMINER'S REPORT

1886-1916. 3 vols. (1917-1920, missing.)

Reports of examination of treasury of Allen County listing amounts and balances. No index. Handwritten and typed on printed forms. Volumes average 100 pages. 16 x 14 x .25. County courthouse. Room 102.

Contracts

348. AUDITOR'S RECORD OF CERTIFIED CONTRACTS
1919-1927. 2 vols.

A record listing name of contractor, name of improvement, and amount. Alphabetically arranged as to names of contractors. Handwritten. Volumes average 125 pages. 15 x 11 x 1. County courthouse.

1919-1927, 1 volume. Room 400A.
1921-1926, 1 volume. Room 102.

349. RECORD
1881-1884. 1 vol.

Architect's estimate of materials, extras, labor, and contracts on the construction of the courthouse. No index. Handwritten on printed forms. 200 pages. 17 x 13 x 2. County courthouse. Room 102.

350. ESTIMATE ON CHILDREN'S HOME CONTRACT
1891-1892. 1 vol.

Architect's estimate of cost of materials, extras, labor and contracts for construction of children's home. No index. Handwritten. 100 pages. 18 x 13 x 1.5. County courthouse. Room 400A.

351. RECORD OF CONTRACTS
1916—. 6 vols. (1930-1935 missing.)

Auditor's record of each contract listing name a contractor, estimate, and remarks. Alphabetical index in front of each volume. Handwritten on printed forms. Volumes average 600 pages. 16 x 14 x 2. County courthouse.

1916-1925, 1927-1929, 4 volumes. Room 102.
1925-1927, 1 volume. Room 202.
1936, 1 volume. Room 100.

Bridge, Ditch, and Road Records

352. BRIDGE RECORD
1898-1913. 4 vols.

A record of appropriations for bridge funds listing name of contractor, name of bridge, and amount in each case. Alphabetical index in front of each volume. Handwritten. Volumes average 300 pages. 16 x 10 x 2. County courthouse.

1898-1905, 1 volume. Room 202.
1906-1909, 2 volumes. Room 400B.
1912-1913, 1 volume. Room 102.

353. DITCH JOURNAL
1887-1931. 3 vols. (1902-1905, missing.)

A record of commissioners' acts affecting ditch improvements. No index. Handwritten. Volumes average 600 pages. 18 x 14 x 2.5. County courthouse. Room 202.

354. DITCH RECORD
1871-1932. 31 vols. (— 1871, missing.)

A record of ditches giving name of each ditch, description of lands affected, and cost. No index. 1871-1908, handwritten; 1908-1932, typed. Volumes average 500 pages. 14 x 10 x 4. County courthouse. Room 202.

355. PUBLIC ROADS
1831-1934. 7 vols. (1840-1851 missing.)

A record listing name of road, name of petitioner, surveyor's report, procedure, and notice in each case. Alphabetical index in front of each volume. Handwritten. Volumes average 600 pages. 18 x 12 x 2.5. County courthouse. Room 202.

356. ROAD REPAIR RECORD
1904-1912. 7 vols.

A record listing cost of repairing of roads, name and address of contractor, description of improvement, and cost. Alphabetical index in front of each volume. Handwritten. Volumes average 450 pages. 16 x 12 x 2. County courthouse.

1904-1905, 3 volumes. Room 102.
1906-1912, 3 volumes. Room 400B.
1911-1912, 1 volume. Room 202.

357. TURNPIKE DIRECTORS' JOURNAL
1903-1921. 2 vols. (— 1903, missing.)

A record of road repairs listing name of roads, description of repair work, and amounts. No index. Typed. Volumes average 300 pages. 18 x 13 x 2. County courthouse. Room 202.

358. WESTWOOD SEWER DISTRICT
1924-1927. 1 vol.

An itemized account of Westwood sewer cost. No index. Handwritten. 300 pages. 14 x 11 x 1. County courthouse. Room 202.

359. ENGINEER'S CERTIFICATES
1884. 1 vol.

Duplicate of surveyor's or engineer's certificates for ditch and road work and other similar work. No index. Handwritten on printed forms. 250 pages. 17 x 11 x 1.5. County courthouse. Room 102.

Licenses and Permits

360. AUDITOR'S DAILY AND MONTHLY REPORT
1925-1931, 1 vol.

A monthly and daily report of motor vehicle population and municipal registration. Chronologically arranged. Typed. Volumes average 300 pages. 17 x 14 x 2. County courthouse. Room 102.

361. INDEX TO MOTOR VEHICLE LICENSES
1926. 1 vol.

An index listing name of each owner, address, and license number. Handwritten. 300 pages. 18 x 14 x 3. County courthouse. Room 102.

362. MOTOR VEHICLE REPORTS, COMPLAINTS HEARD, APPROPRIATIONS
1927-1934. 23 File boxes.

Record of appropriations, complaints heard, and motor vehicle reports listing names, dates, amounts, etc. Cardex system. 17 x 11.5 x 5. County courthouse. Room 202, in steel cabinet.

363. DOG REGISTER
1917-1927. 5 vols.

A registry of dogs listing each owner's name, address, number of dogs, and amount of fees. Alphabetically arranged as to names of owners. Handwritten and typed. Volumes average 400 pages. 16 x 12 x 2. County courthouse.

1917-1918, 1 volume. Room 102.
1919-1927, 4 volumes. Room 202.

364. RECORD OF TRANSFER OF CERTIFICATES OF OWNERSHIP OF DOGS
1927-1929. 1 vol.

A record listing names of parties and description of dogs. Handwritten. Chronologically arranged. 50 pages. 11 x 9 x 1. County courthouse. Room 202.

365. BUILDING PERMITS
1926. 1 vol.

A record listing name, building improvement, description and amount. No index. Handwritten on printed forms. 300 pages. 16 x 10 x 2.5. County courthouse. Room 102.

Special Accounts

366. JOURNAL
1889-1934. 13 vols.

A record of minutes and journal record of various boards of Lima and Allen County. Alphabetical index in front of each volume. Handwritten and typed. Volumes average 250 pages. 18 x 12 x 2. County courthouse.

1889-1903, 4 volumes. Room 400B.
1911-1913, 1916-1924, 4 volumes. Room 102.
1902-1934, 5 volumes. Room 202.

367. SINKING FUND JOURNAL
1920-1928. 4 vols.

A record of proceedings of the board of trustees of sinking funds listing names and amounts. Alphabetical index in front of each volume. Volumes average 300 pages. 14 x 9 x 1.5. County courthouse. Room 202.

368. TOWNSHIP TREASURER'S ACCOUNT
1866-1873. 1 vol.

A record of statements of accounts of the treasurer of the townships, listing receipts, expenditures, and balances. Alphabetical index as to township in front of volume. Handwritten. 250 pages. 18 x 14 x 2. County courthouse. Room 202.

369. BUDGET RECORD
1911-1915. 2 vols.

A record of the annual budget of board of township trustees listing names, funds, and amounts. No index. Typed. Volumes average 300 pages. 18 x 13 x 2. County courthouse.

1911-1913, 1 volume. Room 102.
1914-1915, 1 volume. Room 400A.

370. SHEEP CLAIM BOOK
1882—. 3 vols.

A record listing name of each owner, number of sheep killed, amount claimed, amount allowed, and to whom paid. No index. Handwritten on printed forms. Volumes average 125 pages. 18 x 11 x 1. County courthouse.

1882-1890, 1 volume. Room 102.
1892—, 2 volumes. Room 202.

371. MOTHERS' PENSION RECORDS
1915-1916. 1 vol.

A record of mothers' pensions listing names, addresses, and amounts. Alphabetical index in front of volume. Handwritten. 100 pages. 18 x 18 x 1. County courthouse. Room 400B.

372. SOLDIERS' RELEASE RECORD
1886—. 4 vols.

A record of indigent soldiers, sailors, marines, their wives, widows, and minor children listing names and amount of relief. No index. Handwritten. Volumes average 300 pages. 18 x 14 x 1. County courthouse.

1886-1908, 1 volume. Room 400B.
1884-1908, 1 volume. Room 102.
1908-1915, 1 volume. Room 400A.
1916—, 1 volume. Room 202.

373. SCHOOL DISTRICTS
1839-1958. 1 vol.

A record listing amounts and dates of issue of orders to township treasurers and amount of state and county funds for school purposes. Arranged as to township. Handwritten. 400 pages. 14 x 12 x 1.5. County courthouse. Room 202.

374. AUDITOR'S SETTLEMENT AT SCHOOL FUNDS
1859-1927. 9 vols. (1866-1872 missing.)

A record of auditor's accounts with the school districts of the townships listing names of districts and amounts. No index. Handwritten on printed forms. Volumes average 500 pages. 18 x 12 x 2.5. County courthouse.

1859-1865, 1873-1882, 1884-1927, 7 volumes. Room 202.
1883-1892, 1 volume. 102.

375. RECORD OF SCHOOL LANDS
1851-1881. 1 vol.

A record listing names of school districts, lands, locations, and remarks. No index. Handwritten. 250 pages. 18 x 12 x 2. County courthouse. Room 202.

376. SCHOOL EXAMINER'S RECORD
1866-1875. 1 vol.

A record listing names of applicants, addresses, and grades received. No index. Handwritten. 450 pages. 14 x 11 x 2. County courthouse. Room 202.

377. COMMON SCHOOL LIBRARY
1859-1860. 1 vol.

An account with the state library through which library books were issued through county auditor to various townships in Allen County. Price per volume accompanied list issued, and receipts were given by township clerks. Alphabetical index as to townships in front of volume. Handwritten. 300 pages. 14 x 11 x 2. County courthouse. 202.

Miscellaneous

378. ENUMERATION OF YOUTH
1819-1820. 2 vols.

Original surveys of townships of Allen County, Ohio. One volume is an exact copy of the original and was transcribed in the 1850s. No index in older volumes. Newer one indexed as to range and township numbers. Handwritten. Volumes average 113 pages. 17.5 x 13 x 1.25. County courthouse. Room 202.

379. RECORD THE TOWNSHIP SURVEYS
1831-1836. 1 vol.

A record of surveys made in the various townships of Allen County. No index. Handwritten. 150 pages. 14 x 8 x 1. County courthouse. Room 202.

380. OLD AND NEW LOT NUMBERS, LIMA, OHIO
1831-1873. 1 vol.

A record listing date of recording of old and new lot numbers, Lima, Ohio. Alphabetical index in front of volume. Handwritten. 200 pages. 16 x 12 x 1.5. County courthouse. Room 202.

381. CERTIFICATES OF STOCKS
1918. 1 vol.

Stubs and certificates of stock of Allen County Abstract Company listing names, dates, and amounts. No index. Handwritten on printed forms. 500 pages. 14 x 7 x 2.25. County courthouse. Room 102.

382. LIMA CITY ORDINANCES
1898. 1 vol.

Ordinances and franchises the city of Lima in force in 1898. Alphabetical index in back of volume. Printed. 180 pages. 8 x 6 x .5. County courthouse. Room 202.

383. LIST OF ELECTORS REGISTERED
1905. 1 vol.

Contains a list of all registered voters of Lima, Ohio, by ward and precinct. No index. Printed. 150 pages. 8 x 6 x 1. County courthouse. Room 202.

384. UTILITY REPORT RECORDS
1930-1935. 4 file boxes.

Utility report records listing railroad, telegraph, power plant, telephone, and pipeline transactions. Cardex system. 26 x 17 x 11. County courthouse. Room 100, in steel file cabinet.

385. POOR'S MANUAL OF RAILROADS
1887. 1 vol.

Railroad statistics, mileage, routes, and maps. Alphabetical index in front of volume. Printed. 200 pages. 8 x 6 x 3.5. County courthouse. Room 102.

386. HISTORICAL AND LITERARY CURIOSITIES
1852. 1 vol.

This volume contains facsimilies of documents and letters, broadsides, and newspapers of Revolutionary War period, also silhouettes of outstanding personages of that time. Alphabetical index in front of volume. Printed. 200 pages. 18 x 12 x 2. County courthouse. Room 202.

387. ALLEN COUNTY AGRICULTURAL SOCIETY
1918-1925. 1 vol.

A record of the meetings and elections of the society. No index. Handwritten. 200 pages. 14 x 9 x 1. County courthouse. Room 102.

388. EUROPEAN CORN BORER CONTROL
1927. 1 vol.

A record of facts relative to control of European corn borer. No index. Handwritten on printed forms. 250 pages. 11 x 10 x 1.5. County courthouse. Room 102.

389. MISCELLANEOUS RECORDS
No date. 8 file boxes.

Miscellaneous records of many kinds, predominantly old tax returns. No index. 27 x 12 x 5.5. County courthouse. Room 100, in steel cabinet.

Map and Plat Books

390. CITY MAPS
1920-1926. 50 maps.
Lima ward and township political maps bound and loose-leaf binders. R.H. Gamble, publisher. Scale, 1 inch equals 100 feet. County courthouse. Room 100.

391. MAPS
1909-1901. 24 maps.
Political maps of townships, villages, and subdivisions. J. Cupp, C.E. publisher. Printed. Scale, 1 inch equals 100 feet. Maps average 36 x 23. County courthouse. Room 102, in map case.

392. GRAY'S ATLAS OF THE UNITED STATES
1878. 1 vol.
A historical and geographical data of the United States. Alphabetical index in front of volume. 200 pages. 18 x 14 x 1.5. County courthouse. Room 102.

393. HISTORICAL ATLAS OF ALLEN COUNTY
1880, 1 vol.
An historical and geographical atlas of Allen County, Ohio, containing township maps, and showing ownership of land. Index in front of volume. Printed. 100 pages. 18 x 14 x 1. County courthouse. Room 202.

394. TOWNSHIP PLAT BOOK
1870, 1910, 1926. 22 vols.
Surveyor's plats and assessment records for the townships and taxing districts. 1870, 1910, no index; 1926, alphabetical index in front of volume. Handwritten and hand drawn. Volumes average 42 pages. 17.6 x 13 x .6. County courthouse.
1870, 1810, 18 volumes. Room 102.
1926, 4 volumes. Room 100.

The office of county treasurer, established by an act of the Northwest Territory and 1792, was continued by the state of Ohio. (Pease., *op. cit.*, 68-69.) Although the constitution of 1802 made no provision for the office of county treasurer, it was created by the legislative act of 1803. (1 O.L. 98.) The treasurer, appointed by the associate judges in 1803 and by the county commissioners in 1804 was required to take an oath; give bond for the faithful performance of the duties of his office; and was subject to removal by the appointing power. (1 O.L. 98; 2 O.L. 154.) The treasurer remained an appointed official until 1827, and after that date and elective one by popular vote in the county. (25 O.L. 25-32.) The constitution of 1851, although not specifically creating the office, stated that no person should hold the office of the treasurer or more than four years in any six. *(Ohio Const. 1851*, Art. X, sec. 3. This provision was repealed in 1933, with the adoption of an amendment authorizing any county to adopt a charter form of government.) The legislature, interpreting the constitutional provisions, fixed the term of office at two years in 1859. (59 O.L. 101.) The term of office continued at two years until 1935 when it was extended to four years. (116 O.L. pt. 2, 1st. s. sess H. 603.) Until 1906 the county treasurer received his remuneration from fees, since that date his salary has been determined by law, according to the population of the county.

Although the duties of the treasurer were defined by statute in the earlier period, the act of 1827 and act of 1831, repealing the provision of the latter acts, define his duties in detail. The provisions of the latter acts, although subject to amendment and repeal, furnished the basis for subsequent legislation and laid the basis for the present-day duties of the treasurer, which, in the main, do not differ greatly from those prescribed by the earlier of statutes.

In 1803 the treasurer was given his present-day duty of giving public notice of the tax duplicate. Upon receiving from the county auditor a duplicate of the taxes assessed upon the property of the county, the treasurer prepares notices to be posted in three places in each township, one, the place in which elections are held. Also, the notice is inserted for six consecutive weeks in a newspaper having the greatest circulation in the county. (1 O.L. 96; 29 O.L. 291; 52 O.L. 124.) He receives money in payment of taxes levied for the county, state, and for other purposes; giving the person so paying, a receipt. (G.C. 2650.) (29 O.L. 291; 76 O.L. 70; 85 O.L. 327.) In the earlier years of the office the treasurer was required to give announcement of the time he would be in the respective townships of the county and in his office at the seat of justice to receive tax collections. Since 1858 the treasurer has been authorized to prescribe the semi-annual payment of taxes or assessments levied upon real estate or upon delinquent real estate taxes or assessments. (55 O.L. 62; 56 O.L. 101.) Moreover, since 1908 the commissioners have been authorized to extend the time of paying taxes not more than thirty days after the time fixed by law. (99 O.L. 435; 114 O.L. 730; 115 O.L. pt. 2, 226.)

The treasurer is required to report to the auditor after each semi-annual collection of taxes, showing the amount of taxes received in each taxing district in the county since the last settlement. Since 1904 the semi-annual settlements have been made under the heads of liquor taxes, cigarette taxes, inheritance taxes, delinquent personal taxes, road taxes and general taxes. The treasurer keeps his accounts in books enabling him to compile such reports. (G.C. sec. 2, 643; 29 O.L. 296; 97 O.L. 458.)

After the taxes are collected and immediately after each settlement with the county auditor, the county treasurer, upon the presentation of the proper warrant on the auditor, pays to the township treasurer, city or village treasurer, the treasurer of the school district, or treasurer of any legally constituted board authorized by law to receive the funds or proceeds of any special tax levy, or other officer delegated with authority to receive such funds, all money in the county belonging to such boards and subdivision. (G.C. sec. 2, 689; R.S. 1122; 56 O.L. 101.) Then, too, after the treasurer has made each settlement with the county auditor, he is required to pay to the state treasurer, on warrant from the state auditor, the full amount of all sums found by the state auditor to belong to the state. (56 O.L. 101; 114 O.L. 732.)

The treasurer is required to keep an account current with the county auditor. This practice originated in 1831. Each day the treasurer makes a statement to the county auditor for the previous day's business showing the amount of taxes received on auditor's drafts, the amount received from other sources, together with the amount of money deposited in the depository, the amount paid out by check and by cash, and the balance in the treasury. (G.C. sec. 2, 642; 55 O.L. 44; 97 O.L. 458.)

Another function of the county treasurer, having its inception in the earlier years of the office, is the collection of delinquent taxes. It was, and is, his duty to assess a penalty on the tax duplicate for the non-payment of taxes, which penalty when collected is paid into the treasurer's fund. If the treasurer is unable to collect the delinquent taxes, he is authorized to apply to the clerk of courts of common pleas, and the clerk serves notice to show cause why such taxes were not paid. The court may enter a rule against the delinquent tax payer for the payment and costs and enforce it by attachment. (56 O.L. 175; 99 O.L. 435.)

During the last decade provision has been made whereby delinquent taxes, assessments and penalties charged on the tax duplicate against any entry of real estate may be paid in installments during the five consecutive semi-annual taxpaying periods, whether such real estate has been certified as delinquent or not. (G.C. sec. 2, 672; 114 O.L. 827.) The Whittemore act, past in 1936, provides for the collection of delinquent real estate taxes and assessments, personal property and classified property tax prior to 1935, by installments.(S.B. 359, 1st. s. sess. 35, *Baldwin's Ohio Code Service*, Oct., 1936, 10.) In some of more populous counties the treasurers maintain a separate bureau for the collection of delinquent taxes.

The county treasurer has charge of the funds collected by taxes, and also other funds belonging to the county. Although earlier acts made provisions for storage vaults in the county treasury for county deposits, the commissioners have been authorized, since 1894, to receive sealed bids for the deposit of county funds and the bank or trust companies offering the highest rate of interest are selected as a county depositories. (91 O.L. 403; 102 O.L.60; 115 O.L. pt. 2, 215.)

The treasurer, as well as the sheriff, the prosecutor, and the clerk, is required to report annually to the county commissioners. Since 1874 the county auditor and county commissioners have been required to make a thorough examination of all books, vouchers, accounts, moneys, bonds, securities and other property in the treasury at least every six months. (G.C. sec. 2, 699; R.S. 1129; 71 O.L. 137.) The treasurer, besides being under the supervision of the county commissioners and county auditor, is subject to the supervision of the state auditor. In 1902 an act was passed providing for a uniform system of accounting and auditing for all public offices in the state, under the direction of a bureau of inspection in the office of the state auditor. The act provides, also, for the annual examination of the finance of all public offices. (G.C. sec. 2, 641; 114 O.L. 728; R.S. 1084.)

The treasurer, like other county officials, is required to turn over to his successor all books, papers, moneys, and records appertaining to his office. Since the inception of the office the treasurer has been the official custodian of the bonds furnished to the state by the county auditor, county commissioners, county sheriff, etc. Since 1869, he has been required to record and preserve a record of the deputies appointed and removed by the county auditor. (G.C. sec. 2, 563; 66 O.L. 35.)

The treasurer is a member of the budget commission and the county board of review. (G.C. sec. 5, 625-16; G.C. sec. 5, 580.)

Taxation Records

395. ASSESSMENT RECORDS
1932-1935. 1 vol.
A record listing each owner's name, description of his property, and amount of assessment. Chronological index. Handwritten and typed. 600 pages. 20 x 14 x 2.5. County courthouse. Room 205.

396. SPECIAL ASSESSMENT BOOKS
1846—. 13 vols. (1847-1873, 1876-1881,1884, missing.)
A record listing ditch, sewer, highway, and other special tax assessments. Alphabetically arranged as to range, township, and section. Handwritten. Volumes average 600 pages. 20 x 14 x 2.5. County courthouse.
1846, 1874-1875, 1882-1883, 1885-1888, 9 volumes. Room 400B.
1889—, 4 volumes. Room 203.

397. TAX DUPLICATES
1936. 1 file box.
The 1936 June tax duplicate listing names and amounts. Indexed as to taxing district. 66 x 48 x 10. County courthouse. Room 205.

398. TREASURER'S DUPLICATE REAL ESTATE
1928. 1 vol.
A record listing name of each real estate owner, description of property, and value. Indexed as to range, township, and section. Handwritten. 600 pages. 20 x 14 x 2.5. County courthouse. Room 205.

399. TREASURER'S GENERAL TAX DUPLICATE
1935. 1 vol.
A record listing names of parties, assessments, and payment dates. No index. Typed. 300 pages. 18 x 18 x 1. County courthouse. Room 201.

400. TREASURER'S DUPLICATE
1938—. 250 vols. (1839-1844, 1846-1847, 1849, 1851, 1856, 1860, 1885-1888, 1890, 1900-1920, missing.)
A record of assessed taxes listing names of owners, description of properties, and the value of each. Arranged as to range, township, and section numbers.

Handwritten. Volumes average 300 pages. 18 x 12 x 1.5. County courthouse.

1838-1900, 150 volumes. Room 400.
1921-1930, 71 volumes. Room 205.
1931-1935, 19 volumes. Room 203.
1931-1935, 8 volumes. Room 201.
1934, 2 volumes. Room 201A.

401. TREASURER'S DELINQUENT DUPLICATE
1874. 3 vols. (1875-1921, 1927-1930, missing.)

A record listing name of owner, description of property, value, and amount of tax for each delinquent property. No index. 1874, handwritten; 1922—. Typed. Volumes average 400 pages. 18 x 13 x 25. County courthouse.

1874, 1922-1926, 2 volumes. Room 400B.
1931—, 1 volume. Room 201.

402. PERSONAL AND CLASSIFIED TAX RECORD, 1st HALF OF 1936,
1936. 1 vol.

A record containing owners' names, description of each property, and amount of tax. Alphabetical index in front of volume. Handwritten and typed. 600 pages. 20 x 14 x 2.5. County courthouse. Room 203.

403. TAX RECEIPTS
1890-1906. 5 vols. (1895, 1898-1899, missing.)

Stubs of tax receipts. No index. Handwritten on printed forms. Volumes average 100 pages. 8 x 4 x 1. County courthouse. Room 400B.

404. TREASURER'S INHERITANCE TAX CHARGES
1936. 1 vol.

A record listing names of parties, addresses, and amounts of inheritance tax charges. No index. Typed on printed forms. 100 pages. 12 x 12 x 1.5. County courthouse. Room 201A.

405. TAX RECEIPTS

1936. 840 pigeon holes.

Current tax receipts. 480 pigeon holes, county and village tax receipts; 360 pigeon holes, city tax receipts; listing names, taxing district, and amount. Indexed as to taxing district number. 12 x 4 x 2. County courthouse.

1936, 480 county files. Room 203.

1936, 360 city files. Room 201.

406. TAX RECEIPT STUBS

(various dates.) 35 file boxes.

Old tax receipt stubs listing names and amount paid. Indexed as to taxing district. 5 x 8 x 10. County courthouse. Room 205.

Ledgers and Journals

407. TREASURER'S JOURNAL OF PAYMENTS INTO TREASURY

1933—. 2 vols. (— 1933, missing.)

A record listing name of payor, purpose, amount, and name of fund in case of each payment into treasury. Handwritten. Volumes average 300 pages. 18 x 13 x 2.5. County courthouse. Room 201A.

408. TREASURER'S LEDGER

1905—. 3 vols. (1907-1932, missing.)

A record listing names, dates, and amounts paid. Alphabetical index in front of each volume. Handwritten. Volumes average 450 pages. 18 x 13 x 2.5. County courthouse.

1905-1906, 1 volume. Room 400B .

1933—, 2 volumes. Room 201A.

409. TREASURER'S JOURNAL OF WARRANTS REDEEMED

1934—. 2 vols.

A record listing name, purpose, number of warrant, and the amount of each redeemed warrant. No index. Handwritten. Volumes average 250 pages. 18 x 13 x 2. County courthouse. Room 201A.

410. TREASURER'S COURT WARRANTS
1877—. 2 vols. (1882-1930, missing.)

A record listing names of parties, name of court, amount of fees, and date of each court warrant. No index. Handwritten on printed forms. Volumes average 300 pages. 18 x 13 x 2.5. County courthouse.

1877-1881, 1 volume. Room 400B.
1931—, 1 volume. Room 201A.

411. DAILY CASH BALANCE
1932—. 1 vol.

Record of cash receipts, disbursements, and the cash balance. Chronological index. Handwritten on printed forms. 600 pages. 16 x 12 x 3. Phone 201A.

412. TREASURER'S CASH BOOK
1860—. 6 vols. (1863-1869, 1879-1881, 1885-1902, 1906-1915, 1918-1924, missing.)

A record of cash accounts of treasurer listing dates, amount of receipts, disbursements, and the balance. No index. Handwritten. Volumes average 300 pages. 18 x 13 x 2.5. County courthouse.

1860-1862, 1 volume. Room 400A.
1870-1878, 1882-1884, 1903-1905, 1916-1917, 4 volumes. Room 400B.
1924—, 1 volume. Room 201A.

413. RECORD OF SALES TAX COLLECTION
1931-1935. 1 large file.

A record of sales taxes. Index in folders as to years. 60 x 54 x 14.

414. VENDOR'S PURCHASE ORDER
1935—. 6 file boxes.

Treasurer's copy of the vendor's purchase orders. Alphabetically arranged. 18 x 10 x 6. County courthouse. Room 205.

415. MISCELLANEOUS PAPERS
1932—. 25 file boxes.

Old papers of various kinds, tax dubs, releases, daily reports, reports of cigarette stubs, etc. Cardex system. File boxes average 7 x 10 x 20. County courthouse. Room 201A.

The county board of education, a modern administrative and supervisory agency developed during the last two decades, supplanted the smaller educational units, which, established during the earlier period of Ohio history, became inefficient and unable to meet the modern requirements as demanded by rural communities.

During the earlier period of Ohio history educational administration, due to the newness of the state, the sparseness of the population, and the undeveloped means of transportation was, by necessity, local in character. For fourteen years after the admission of Ohio as a state, though the constitution stated that means of education should be encouraged by the general assembly, no legislation was enacted for public schools. (*Ohio Const. 1802*, Art. VIII, sec. 3, 25, 27.) It was not until 1817 that the legislature authorized six or more people in the townships to form associations to build school houses and to be incorporated for educational purposes. (15 O.L. 407.) This was a beginning, but as yet the values of an educational system were not readily perceived by those engaged in subduing a stubborn wilderness.

The first permanent law for the organization of schools in Ohio was passed in 1821. Under the provisions of this act, the electors of the township were authorized to vote on the proposition of dividing the townships into school districts. If the proposition carried three school commissioners were to be elected, who, in turn, were authorized to select a clerk and a collector who should act as a treasurer. They were authorized, also, to levy taxes for the support of schools and to hire teachers. (19 O.L. 54.)

As education began to advance in the early years of the nineteenth century, some kind of state control was needed. Accordingly, in 1837, the office of state superintendent of schools was established. A year later an act was passed making the county auditor also the county superintendent of schools and, in each township the clerk was made superintendent of the smaller unit. The county superintendent was made responsible to the state superintendent in all educational affairs. In the same year each incorporated city, town or borough, not regulated by a charter was made a separate school district. The voters in each division were authorized to elect three directors. (31 O.L. 21.) The effectiveness of this organization, however, was destroyed in 1840, when the legislature abolished the office of state superintendent and the secretary of state took over his functions of tabulating and transmitting school statistics. (38 O.L. 130.) Seven years later, twenty-five counties were allowed to have county superintendents, and in 1848 the provision of the previous act were extended to all counties in the state. (46 O.L. 86.)

Although marked changes were made in the curriculum of the schools, the history of education in Ohio from 1850 to the early part of the twentieth century was largely one of the gradual transference of powers from districts to townships, and from townships to county in the interest of a better system of education. It was not, however, until within the last three decades that the county became the unit for educational administration. (70 O.L. 195, 204; 97 O.L. 354.)

The first permanent law for the establishment of the county board of education, through the county superintendent was known as early as 1838, was enacted in 1914. Under this act the school districts were classified, and provision was made for a county school district, exclusively of the territory embraced in any city or village desiring exemption. The county district was to be under the supervision of five board members elected by the presidents of the village and rural school boards. The members were to hold office for one, two, three, four, and five years respectively, and each year one member was to be selected.

The county board of education was authorized to change school district lines, afford transportation for children living more than two miles from a school house; appoint a county superintendent; and certify annually to the county auditor the number of teachers and superintendents employed, their salaries, and the amount apportioned of for each school district. The county superintendent, acting as secretary of the board, was required to keep a full record of the proceedings of the board properly indexed, in a book provided for that purpose. Each motion with the person making it and the vote thereon, was to be entered on the record. (104 O.L. 133; 108 O.L. pt. 1, 704.)

The county was divided into administrative divisions containing one or more villages or rural school districts. Each district was to be under the supervision of a district superintendent who was required to visit the schools in his charge; direct and assist teachers in the performance of their duties; and classify and control promotions of pupils. Moreover he was required to report annually to the county superintendent on matters under his charge, assemble teachers for the purpose of conferring on curricular matters, discipline and school management. (104 O.L. 133-145.)

Significant changes were made by the act of 1920. Under it the county board members became elective. They were authorized to appoint one or more assistant county superintendents for a term of three years. The board was authorized to publish, with the advice and consent of the county superintendent, a minimum course of study to serve as a guide to local board members. The same act abolished the office of district superintendent. (G.C. sec. 4, 728-1, 4, 729; 108 O.L. pt. 1, 706.)

The county organization has placed the rural schools on a plan of equality with the city schools. The consolidation of smaller units has eliminated the small, ill-equipped schools, and provides under one roof facilities and instruction suited to the needs of the rural children under the supervision of educational specialists.

Reports

416. REGISTRATION AND ATTENDANCE RECORD
1900—. 6 file boxes.
A registration and attendance record of all pupils in Allen County schools listing names, schools, days present, days absent, and date registered. Cardex system. 17 x 7 x 6.5. County courthouse. Room 305B.

417. RECORDS OF ATTENDANCE
1878—. 14 file drawers.
Attendance records of all pupils in Allen County schools listing names, schools, days present, and days absent. Cardex system. Cabinet size, 48 x 25 x 15. County courthouse. Room 305B.

418. ANNUAL AND MONTHLY SCHOOL REPORTS
1878—. 8 file boxes.
Annual and monthly reports from teachers of Allen County schools. Cardex system. 15 x 11 x 5. County courthouse. Room 305B.

419. ATTENDANCE RECORD
1879—. 40 vols.
Registers of enrollment and attendance of pupils of Allen County schools listing names, addresses, schools, days present, and days absent. No index. Handwritten on printed forms. Volumes average 100 pages. 12 x 12 x .5. County courthouse. Room 305B.

Examinations

420. RECORD OF EXAMINATIONS
1878-1915. 2 vols. (— 1878, missing.)
A record of school examinations in Allen County with remarks and suggestions. No index. Handwritten. Volumes average 400 pages. 17 x 12 x 2. County courthouse. Room 305B.

One of the recent developments in county health administration has been the establishment of the general health district, or county health department. As an act of the legislature, in 1919, the townships and municipalities in each county, exclusive of any city having a population of 25,000 were to constitute a general health district. Cities having a population of 25,000 or more were to constitute a municipal health district. On the other hand, where municipalities of not less than 10,000 or more than 25,000 which maintained a board of health meeting the qualifications as set by the legislative act, were authorized, after examination by the state health department, to continue operation as a separate health district. (108 O.L. pt. 1, 238.) An amendment passed in December 1919, made each city a health district. The townships and villages in each county were combined into a general health district. Provision was also made whereby a city and general health district might combine for administrative purposes. (108 O.L. pt. 2, 1086.)

Under the latter act, the provisions of which are still in force, the mayor of each municipality, not constituting a city health district, and the chairman of the trustees of each township were authorized to meet at the seat of justice and organize by selecting a chairman and a secretary. The organization, known as the district advisory council, selects and appoints a district board of health composed of five members one of whom must be a physician. The members serve without compensation. (*Ibid.*, 1085.)

Within thirty days after their appointment the members of the district or "county board of health" organize by selecting one of their members as president and another member as president pro-tempore. The board is authorized to appoint a licensed physician as district health commissioner. This officer, serving as secretary to the board, is designated as deputy state registrar of vital statistics, and is required to report monthly to the state registrar of vital statistics. (G.C. sec. 1, 261-32; 108 O.L. pt. 1, 242.)

The duties of the county board of health include, among other things, the appointment, upon the recommendation of the health commissioner, of a "whole - time" public health nurse, a clerk, and such additional public health nurses, physicians and other persons as may be necessary for the proper conduct of its work. Moreover, the board makes a study of the prevalence of disease within the county, communicable diseases, provides for the treatment of venereal diseases, inspection of public charitable, benevolent, correctional and penal institutions. In addition to this, the board may provide inspection of dairies, stores, restaurants, hotels, and other places where food is manufactured, handled, stored, sold or offered for sale. (108 O.L. pt. 2, 1088-1089.) The Board is authorized to make any and all regulations it deems necessary for the prevention or restriction of disease, and the prevention, abolition or suppression of nuisance. (108 O.L. pt. 2, 1069.) The county prosecutor represents the board and legal matters. (which see.)

The board may provide for carrying on such laboratory work as may be necessary for the conduct of its work. It may establish a laboratory or contract with existing laboratories for the performance of its work. All state institutions, supplied in whole or in part by public funds, must furnish such laboratory service to a county board of health under the terms agreed upon. (108 O.L. pt. 2, 1089.)

The work of health department is financed by public taxation. The board annually estimates, in itemized form, the amount needed for the next fiscal year. Such estimates, certified by the county auditor, are submitted to the county budget commissioners which may reduce any items in such an estimate, but cannot increase any item or the aggregate of all items. The aggregate amount, as fixed by the budget commissioners, is apportioned by the county health district on the basis of taxable valuations in such townships and municipalities. (*Ibid.*, 1091.)

Minutes and Reports

421. RECORD OF MINUTES OF OFFICIAL BOARD MEETINGS
1919. 2 vols.

A record of official meetings of the board of health. No index. Handwritten. Volumes average 300 pages. 14 x 9 x 1. County courthouse. Room 108B.

422. RECORD OF COUNCIL MEETINGS
1920—. 1 vol.

An official record of minutes of advisory council meetings. No index. Handwritten. 300 pages. 14 x 8 x 1. County courthouse. Room 108B.

423. REPORT RECORDS
1920-1935. 1 file box.

Monthly and annual reports of the activities of board of health. Cardex system. 26 x 14 x 11. County courthouse. Room 108B.

Vital Satistics

424. BIRTH RECORD
1920—. 54 vols.

Copies of original birth certificates listing name, date and place of birth, names and residence of parents. Chronologically arranged. Handwritten. Volumes average 100 pages. 8 x 7 x .75. County courthouse. Room 108.

425. REPORT RECORDS, BIRTHS
1920-1935. 1 file box.

Copies of original birth certificates listing name, date of birth, place of birth, parent's names and addresses. Cardex system; also indexed by separate volumes, see entry 427. 26 x 14 x 11. County courthouse. Room 108B.

426. BIRTHS
1920—. 2 file boxes.

Birth report cards listing each name, date, and place of birth, name and residence of parents. Cardex system; also indexed by separate volumes, see entry 427. 23 x 7 x 5.5. County courthouse. Room 108B.

427. RECORD INDEX
1922—. 2 vols.

An index to records of copies of original birth certificates, see entry 425. Handwritten. Volumes average 152 pages. 14 x 11 x 5. County courthouse. Room 108B.

428. DEATHS
1920-1935. 4 file boxes.

Record of each death in Allen County listing name, address, date, and cause. Cardex system. 23 x 7 x 5.5. County courthouse. Room 108B.

429. RECORD OF PUPILS
1922—. 4 file boxes.

Physical and social records of pupils of various schools and grades in Allen County listing each name, address, school, grade, and report on physical condition. Cardex system. File boxes average 20 x 8.5 x 5.75. County courthouse. Room 108.

430. COMMUNICABLE DISEASES
1920—. 14 file boxes.
Report cards of communicable diseases listing names, addresses, and diseases. Cardex system. 23 x 7 x 5.5. County courthouse. Room 108B.

431. DISEASES
1920—. 3 file boxes.
Report cards used as records of various diseases listing name of person, address, date, and the name of disease. Cardex system. 23 x 7 x 5.5. County courthouse. Room 108B.

432. TUBERCULOSIS CARDS
1920—. 1 file box.
Report cards used as a record of each tuberculosis case, listing name, address, and remarks about the case. Cardex system. 23 x 7 x 5.5. County courthouse. Room 108.

433. REPORT RECORDS, LETTERS ETC
1920-1935. 1 file box.
Duplicates of official letters and tuberculosis files. Cardex system. 26 x 14 x 11. County courthouse. Room 108V.

Old age pensions, although well known in Europe at the end of the nineteenth and beginning of the twentieth century and in a few American states during the same period were not provided for in Ohio until recently. (Arthur Lyon Cross, *A Short History of England and Greater Britain*, N.Y., 1925, 746-747; J. Salwin Schapiro, *Modern and Contemporary European History 1815-1925*, N.Y. 1923, 295.) During the depression years the sight of thousands of aged persons who had lost their homes and savings, and, as a result of such losses faced starvation, touched the sensibilities of Ohioans. Accordingly in1933, an "Old Age Pension" law, proposed by initiative petition, was voted upon at the general election of that year providing for the granting of aid to the aged in Ohio under certain conditions. The law was adopted by a majority of the electors voting thereon. (115 O.L. pt. 2, 431-439.) The act, as amended in 1936, provides, among other things, that any person sixty-five years of age or upward (excluding persons confined in any penal or corrective institution or the state hospital) who is a citizen of the United States, who has resided in Ohio not less than five years during the nine prior to making applications for aid, and, who has resided in the county, wherein application for aid is made, for one year, is eligible to receive a pension, providing his income from all and every source does not exceed $360 per year. (116 O.L. pt. 2, 1st s. sess. H. 605; 116 O.L. pt. 2, s. sess. H. 558.) Moreover the applicant must be unable to support himself, and have no husband, wife, child, or other person who is legally responsible for his support. (115 O.L. pt. 2, 431-439.) In addition to this, the net value of all real and personal property of the applicant, if single, less all incumbrance and liens, must not exceed $3,000; or if married the net value of the property of husband and wife shall not exceed $4,000. (115 O.L. pt. 2, 431-39.) It may be required that such property, as a condition precedent to payment of aid, be transferred to the division of aid for the aged in trust. This provision does not, however, prohibit the applicant or his wife from occupying such property during their lifetime.

For the purpose of administrating the old age pension law there was created in the department of public welfare a division of aid for the aged. The chief of the division of the aid for the aged, appointed by the director of public welfare with the approval of the governor, is authorized to appoint all necessary assistance, clerks, stenographers, and other employees and fix their salaries, subject to approval of the director of public welfare. (115 O.L. pt. 2, 431-439.)

In each county the commissioners constitute a board for administrating the act. However, if the commissioners, by a majority vote, decline to serve in such a capacity, the state director is authorized, with the consent of the director of public welfare, to appoint a board consisting of three or five members, who, like the commissioners, serve without compensation. The local boards are required to keep such reports as the division may prescribe, and is authorized to employ, subject to the approval of the division, such investigators, clerks and other employees as are necessary for the performance of its duties. (*Ibid.*, pt. 2, 431-439.)

Applications for relief are made annually to the local board. Each applicant is thoroughly investigated. In its investigations the local board is not bound by common law or statutory rules of evidence, but is authorized to make investigations in such a manner as seems "best calculated to conform to substantial justice." For the purpose of its investigations, each county board has the power to compel the attendance and testimony of witnesses. Decisions of the local boards may be appealed to the division. (116 O.L. pt. 2, 431-439.)

After the applicants have been investigated by the local board, "certificates of aid" are granted to persons entitled to relief in conformity with the provisions of the law. Each certificate containing the applicant's name and the pension allowed, as well as the records pertaining to the investigation, is forwarded to the division. The division may approve, modify, or reject the certificate and findings of the board. (115 O.L. pt. 2, 435.)

Under the provisions of this act the state became the general guardian of public and private welfare. The pension system relieves the ever-increasing burdens placed upon county infirmaries, which, under the most favorable conditions, are a poor substitute for homes. Although $2,625,000 was appropriated by the legislature for old age pensions in the early part of 1935, the cost of the public in the long run, should not be much greater than the antiquated system of support in charitable institutions. (116 O.L. 510.)

434. APPLICATION FOR OLD AGE PENSIONS, CASE ALLOWED
1934—. 2 file boxes.

Record of applications for old age pensions and cases allowed, listing names, dates, and complete history of each applicant. Cardex system. 23 x 13 x 11.5. County courthouse. Room 103.

435. APPLICATIONS PENDING
1934—. 5 file boxes.

A record of applications pending, listing names, dates, with place for investigations. Cardex system. File boxes average 23 x 17 x 8. County courthouse. Room 103.

436. APPLICATION RECORD
1934—. 1 vol.
A record listing names and addresses of applicants, dates, and disposition of cases. No index. Handwritten. 250 pages. 14 x 10 x 1.5. County courthouse. Room 103.

Accounts

437. ACCOUNTS
1936. 2 vols.
A record of Allen County relief expenditures of various kinds, such as food, medicine, and fuel. (One volume gives a record of voucher numbers and expenses.) One volume has tabular index; other has none. Handwritten. Volumes average 200 pages. 12.5 x 10 x 1. O.P.O. Building, Allen County Relief office.

438. Journal
1936. 1 vol.
A journal of accounts of Allen County relief administration expenditures listing date, amount, and purpose of each. Chronologically arranged. Handwritten. 200 pages. 12 x 8 x 1.5. O.P.O. Building, Allen County Relief office.

Case Records

439. CASE HISTORIES
1935—. 24 file boxes.
Case histories of each relief client listing name, date, age, number in family, former employment, and kind. Started under CWA, transferred to FERA, later transferred to Allen County Relief. These are active and closed cases. Alphabetically arranged as to names of clients. 25 x 13 x 12. O.P.O. Building, Allen County Relief office.

440. ACTIVE CASES
1936. 4 file boxes.
Original papers and cards pertaining to active relief cases in Allen County. File boxes average 20.5 x 12.75 x 11. O.P.O. Building, Allen County Relief office.

441. POSTING CARDS
1936. 2 file boxes.
Cards pertaining to county relief cases listing names, dates, and posting of amounts received. Alphabetically arranged. 18 x 13 x 10. O.P.O. Building, Allen County Relief office.

442. ALLEN COUNTY CLOSED
1936. 2 file boxes
Record pertaining to closed relief cases listing name, number in family, address, and date closed. Cardex system. 18 x 12.5 x 11. O.P.O. Building, Allen County Relief office.

443. CORRESPONDENCE
1936. 1 file box.
Correspondence relating to Allen County relief. Cardex system. 23 x 13 x 11. O.P.O. Building, Allen County Relief office.

Case Records

444. CHILDREN RECEIVED
1914—. 1 vol.
A complete record of children received at county home listing date received, name, date of birth, and all other known facts about each child. Alphabetical index in front of volume. Handwritten. 250 pages. 18 x 16 x 2. Office of Children's Home.

445. CHILDREN RELEASED
1914—. 1 vol.
A record of release of children from custody of children's home listing names, dates, and cause of release. Alphabetical index in front of volume. Handwritten. 250 pages. 16 x 14 x 2. Office of Children's Home.

446. CHILDREN RECEIVED AND RELEASED
1914—. 30 file boxes.
Record of population of home listing name, date received, and date released. Cardex system. 8 x 4 x 4. Office of Children's Home.

447. POPULATION

1914—. 6 file boxes.

A record of population of children's home listing names and giving personal history. Cardex system. 23 x 11 x 16. Office of Children's Home.

Disbursements and Receipts

448. RECEIPTS AND EXPENDITURES

1920—. 3 vols.

A record of money received and amount expended for maintenance of the institution listing dates, amounts, fund, and purpose of expenditure. Alphabetical index in front of each volume. Handwritten. Volumes average 300 pages. 16 x 14 x 1.5. Office of Children's Home.

All addresses refer to Lima, Ohio, unless otherwise noted

Allen County Children Services
123 West Spring Street
https://www.allencsb.com

Allen County Council on Aging
700 North Main Street
https://www.accoa.org/

Allen County Public Health
219 E. Market Street
https://www.allencountypublichealth.org/about-us/board-of-health/

Auditor
301 North Main Street
Rooms 103-107
https://www.allencountyohauditor.com/

Board of Education
204 North Main Street
https://www.allen.boe.ohio.gov/

Clerk of Courts
301 North Main Street
Room 209A
https://clerkofcourts.allencountyohio.com/

Commissioners' Office
204 North Main Street
Suite 301
https://commissioners.allencountyohio.com/

Engineer's Office
1501 North Sugar Street
https://allencountyohengineer.com/

Probate Court and Juvenile Court
1000 Wardhill Avenue
https://allenohioprobate.com/probate-clerks-office/

Prosecutor's Office
204 North Main Street
http://allencountyprosecutor.net/

Recorder's Office
301 North Main Street
Room 204
https://www.allencountyohio.com/recorder

Relief Administration (*see* Need Help Paying Bills - online only)
https://www.needhelppayingbills.com/html/contact-us.html

Sheriff
333 North Main Street
https://acso-oh.us/

Treasurer
301 North Main Street
Room 203
https://allencountyohtreasurer.com/

Additional Allen County information

www.FamilySearch.org
A free website containing many online records for Allen County including Clerk of Courts, Common Pleas, Probate, Recorder, Auditor, Coroner, and Sheriff.

Bowling Green State University
Jerome Library 5th floor, Center for Archival Collections
Bowling Green, Ohio
https://www.bgsu.edu/library/cac.html
The repository for 19 northwestern Ohio counties. Information is not online and must be visited in person.

Allen County Chapter, Ohio Genealogical Society
Website in process
Email: **allencoogs@gmail.com**
Contact the chapter for location of library/holdings. Chapters may have many transcribed court records and may also have cemetery transcriptions as well as local newspapers.

www.Ancestry.com
A pay site containing millions of records. This is available for free at the Main Library, 650 West Market Street, Lima, Ohio. (Not available at Allen County Public Library branches.)

Numbers refer to entry number

Heritage Books by Jana Sloan Broglin:

Additions and Corrections to the W.P.A. Inventory of Adams County, Ohio: West Union

Additions and Corrections to the W.P.A. Inventory of Allen County, Ohio: Lima

Additions and Corrections to the W.P.A. Inventory of Fulton County, Ohio: Wauseon

Additions and Corrections to the W.P.A. Inventory of Lucas County, Ohio: Toledo

Hookers, Crooks and Kooks, Part I: Hookers

Hookers, Crooks and Kooks, Part II: Crooks and Kooks

Lucas County, Ohio, Index to Deaths, 1867–1908

Mason County, Kentucky Wills and Estates, 1791–1832, Second Edition

www.ingramcontent.com/pod-product-compliance
Lightning Source LLC
LaVergne TN
LVHW050647100826
845148LV00011B/2018

* 9 7 8 0 7 8 8 4 2 7 6 6 4 *